# *The* Voice I Couldn't Ignore

GOD TOLD ME HE WAS TAKING MY CHILD.
SEVEN YEARS LATER, HE DID.

**JOHANNA FRANK**

Marrow Publishing
The Voice I Couldn't Ignore
By Johanna Frank

Copyright © 2025, Johanna Frank. *All rights reserved.*

This book is a work of creative nonfiction. It is based on real events, experiences, and personal accounts, drawn from the author's life and spiritual journey. While every effort has been made to accurately portray these events, certain details—such as names, timelines, locations and dialogue—have been adjusted or reconstructed to protect privacy, enhance narrative clarity, and maintain readability.

Spiritual impressions, dreams, and visions have been presented as they were experienced and interpreted by the author. These elements are offered as personal testimony and are not intended as doctrinal statements.

No part of this book may be reproduced by any means, stored in a retrieval system, or transmitted in any form—electronic, audio recording, mechanical, photocopy—without the prior permission of the author.

Trigger warnings—a hatchet murder, a ghostly visitation, a lingering trauma from physical violation, a devastating diagnosis, and a child's death, followed by imprisoning grief and a wrestling with God for control.
Eventually, a transformation of faith.
www.JohannaFrankAuthor.com

Acknowledgments, immense gratitude to:
Deirdre Lockhart, Brilliant Cut Editing – editing and inspiration
Damonza – cover design and interior formatting
My husband – a reliable, steadfast source of strength
David James Photography – back cover photograph (2008) used with permission
Family and Friends – encouragement extraordinaire
Each and every reader! Without you, the question begs—why do this?

ISBN;
978-1-7382907-5-8 Paperback
978-1-7382907-7-2 Kindle
978-1-7382907-8-9 eBook
978-1-7382907-6-5 Audio

Nonfiction – Creative Memoir
Christian Living / Grief

For Adonai,
the Triune God

Dedicated to caregivers everywhere,
—home-based or institutional, hired or volunteered
—with physical, emotional, cognitive, or social specialties
—particularly, those caring for one's spirit
—and even more particularly, mothers and fathers who have lost a child to death.

*"Truly I tell you, whatever you did for one of the least of these brothers and sisters of mine, you did for me."*

—Matthew 25:40b

*Dear Reader,*

*It has taken me well over a decade to piece together unusual happenings with God's abundant sense of mystery. Fifteen years to be precise, since the passing of my teenage daughter, whom, for the purposes of this book, I refer to lovingly as Sadie.*

*This story is based on true events. The prologue reflects knowledge handed down through generations, from mother to child, over a century ago. Everything else—coincidences, dreams, and visions—happened as described. While I've fictionalized the characters and modified some timelines, conversations between the main characters have all been reconstructed from memory. Several exact and taken from preserved journals. Discussions among classmates within the final chapters were created to maintain the spirit and tone of my visit to the Holy Land.*

*My purpose for sharing this personal experience boils down to a simple message. God communicates in many ways. Often, he even catches us off guard. It's when we crawl into that upper room inside ourselves that we can hear what he wants us to hear, see what he wants us to see. It's there, with his Son in our hearts, we feel the breeze of his Spirit. We discover the business that he'll go to great lengths to accomplish. He wants—deeply desires—our agreement to allow him to lift our souls, to join his family.*

*Compelled to share this, I present to you The Voice I Couldn't Ignore, a creative nonfiction work. When a window opens, the breeze can find you. Though don't be misguided, sometimes it takes a whole lot of courage to accept the winds of change. Even so, we can wholeheartedly trust that God is already at work in our stories.*

*With gratitude that you have chosen to open these pages, I thank you for walking alongside.*

*Johanna*

Shall any beginning exist without a curse?

# PROLOGUE

A generational story grounded in facts, wrapped in fiction, and delivered with mystery.

*Ancestor Liesel, Old Yugoslavia, 1922*

FATHER BLED TO death on the kitchen floor.

Mother, desperate to save him, couldn't lift him, so he writhed from the deep cuttings.

Liesel shook and clamped her hand to her mouth.

Mother wrapped his shoulder in cheesecloth. "Liesel! Fetch the brandy," she released the entire instruction in a single exhale.

Liesel's legs moved mechanically around Grandmother's hysterical screaming. Grandmother watched it all. Witnessed a hatchet slash her son on the front porch, wielded by Jake, their neighbor from across the road. The coveting sort, Jake stank of damp soil no matter the buffer Liesel was sure to place between them when passing on the road. Grandmother always did her utmost to "keep his evil personage out of our house."

Barely there with the whooshing in her head about to carry her off, Liesel placed the half-full brandy bottle in her mother's hand.

Father's eyes were blinking and rolling. His mouth was

forming something. Nothing exited but blowing groans and whimpers.

Mother rested his head on her lap, and the swelling belly carrying the new baby rounded against his face as she attempted to stop the bleeding with her apron. It didn't. She nodded at Liesel. "Hold up your apron." When Liesel did, Mother soaked it in brandy and stuffed a section into the corner of his mouth.

His lips closed upon it, and he shut his eyes. His chest rose like it got stuck halfway. He fought the collapse.

Liesel counted. Three blood-soaked areas, each mixed with threads of his shirt. Three attacks deep into his flesh. Across the top of his right arm, in his upper back above his right shoulder blade, and right in the chest. Where his heart is, or was, she thought anyway.

Their village physician bolted in from the front porch but paused to catch his balance after his footing slid in blood. The splays of red seemed to distract his urgency. He gaped at Mother hugging Father's head, then treaded straight to her.

"Stop screaming, woman, and get me some towels," he told Grandmother.

Grandmother didn't want to leave her son's side, so Liesel scrambled for more linens. Father must still be alive. She wasn't sure what dead looked like, so how would she know?

The doctor didn't even open his bag. He just kept the towels as tight as possible against Father's cuts.

Three soldiers from the rural police force arrived. Sweating inside their long wool coats, they tramped into the kitchen, one behind the other, with rifles pointing.

Mother's gaze caught Liesel's, and she nodded toward the sideboard.

Knowing what she meant, Liesel backed up to stand in front

of their family Bible. Using her body, she kept it hidden from the military's view. And, as standard course, she cast a still look downward as though intrigued by her worn, handmade slippers.

"The fields. He's gone to the fields!" Grandmother waved for them to leave, to do their job—go after the man responsible for this absurd attack. Since the fall of the Empire, so much had changed, and she still refused to respect this new regime.

Liesel raised her face. A telling paleness had sallowed their skin. Indeed, none of these soldiers had ever seen such horror. Another screeching demand rose from Grandmother's tongue, and all three of them bolted to the fields where several villagers had already taken to chasing Jake.

"They'll get him," Liesel said. They had to. "Then they'll lock him up in Belgrade."

Grandmother cussed, disgusted by Liesel's obedient nature, probably.

Liesel turned the stove off. No sense boiling the potatoes any longer. Their Sunday pork was still roasting. "Mother, should I turn off the oven?"

Mother wiped her face with the back of her hand and nodded. Father's blood dripped off her chin on account of her tears. There was nothing left to do. Just sit beside Father till his chest stopped moving.

Mother talked to him the whole time. "Ya should'a just kept quiet, minded yer own business." Her shaky fingers dotted his forehead with whatever clean section she could find on her bloody apron. "If that Jake wanted to treat his young wife poorly, that weren't yer doing to fix."

Father was always trying to redeem the man. "We need to get that dark out of him," he'd say, claiming there was light in every soul.

Yesterday, the roads had been muddy, and Jake's wagon wheels got stuck in front of their homestead. Jake took to cursing and swearing at his wife. Father went out to help free the wagon. Now, Mother went on about how Father shouldn't have told Jake he ought not talk that way to his young wife, yelling and cussing at her the way he did. Of course, Jake said he'd talk to his wife however he darned pleased, but apparently, Mother thought that's what enraged Jake.

Grandmother paced, muttering the whole time. "Never liked that Jake."

Well, he didn't care for her much either. He used to call her a busybody. She shouldn't have poked at him today, though, telling him what a fool he was to be wearing a heavy coat on such a warm summer day.

Liesel shivered now. That's when Jake told Father to pass the child on his lap over to Grandmother. Father must have sensed Jake was wanting to fight, so he stood, perhaps thinking he could calm things. Then Jake yanked the ax from inside his coat and began butchering.

Liesel wiped clean her yowling young brother. Then she got another cloth. "Here, Grandmother."

"What are you thinking, girl?" Grandmother swatted the cloth away. "I'll not be washing myself. That's *my son's* blood spattered, and it's all I have left of him. I won't wash till they catch the bugger."

Liesel scooped up the cloth. The floor was such a mess it'd soil quick. "Should you be saying things like that, Grandmother?" It wasn't proper talk. But Liesel held her tongue silent on that part.

"Blood cries for vengeance. Learn it, girl." Grandmother scowled, then moved to the window. "Maybe the villagers will get to him first. They'll kill him if they do."

Liesel crowded in beside her. Not that she expected to see anything, nothing but fields and the trampled marks of a desperate search.

But word came the next morning.

Otto was on their step. Still wearing his church suit, he clutched his good hat against his chest. "Those rural police got to him first." He bunched up the dirt-trodden felt, twisting it like he was wringing a chicken's neck. "They nabbed him, found him crouching like a weasel through black dirt, amid the wheat behind yer place. We didn't get to do what… what we should've. What he deserves."

He opened his fingers, and the hat fell, dropped limp to the no-longer bloody floor, the life wrung from it.

"He'll go to jail, Margarete," he promised Mother. Her shoulders sank, burdened by the weight of it all.

Grandmother snorted. "What's jail? He's still alive. And our lives are forever changed."

Her prediction stood true. Mother lost the baby she was carrying, likely on account of the toiling on the farm. Some women told her that was a blessing. Their husbands helped out at first. But Mother said the family would have to figure it out on their own and there was no use getting accustomed to free help. Liesel took care of the housework, the hot noon meals, and her three younger siblings. Grandmother sat in her rocking chair on the front porch, snoring, because all night long she'd muttered away the events of that dreaded day. It was always fresh in her head. Jail was far too good for the devil, even death, she said, promising to haunt him for the rest of eternity.

Eighteen months later, Jake was freed. Liesel never would understand why. All she knew was everything was changing.

Laws, flags, her siblings' schoolbooks. And he moved straight back in with his parents and wife across the road.

Rumor had it he'd gone crazy, that he spent many mornings at Father's grave site hollering, "Leave me alone!"

Maybe Father was haunting him.

Jake made a point to walk past their front porch each day too, real slow and deliberate, his chest poked high, his hatchet swinging at his side. He mocked Grandmother like a cruel predator toying with his victim. Often, like now, there'd be a screaming match. Grandmother was calling him a murderer. Jake hollered back his usual dire warning: "You'd better keep an eye open. I'm coming back to get the rest of yer family. Every single one." He strutted closer and waved the ax-head like a fist. "I'll butcher 'em all, I swear."

"You're the devil yerself, you are!" Grandmother blasted the words so fierce, Liesel could imagine them emerging with a fire to scorch him.

And he smirked. "I heard that, woman. I'm telling the police how you been tormenting me."

Two hours later, those men in their gray wool coats and leather belts came knocking. Mother answered. The tallest one stepped forward. "Ma'am, you'd best keep your mother-in-law quiet. Harassment is unlawful, you know, particularly the religious sort."

Spring, though, had a way of unwrapping a harsh winter. Grandmother passed in her sleep, though she remained unwilling to surrender her guard on the front porch. At least that's what Liesel figured. Her rocking chair moved on its own as if she were still in it, rifle at her side, muttering curses directed at Jake's farm.

When a traveling caravan of gypsies made their way through town, Liesel hid her siblings in Grandmother's empty bedroom and joined her mother to see what wares they'd offer this go-around. Not that the family had a dollar to spare, but they always purchased something so the gypsies wouldn't cast a curse on their home. 'Course they'd already been cursed, so what would it matter if they did? She was already having recurring nightmares—a striking blow from Jake's hatchet. Over and over. She didn't mind that Grandmother guarded the house in spirit form.

A lone gypsy woman came to the porch and scrutinized Grandmother's rocker.

Liesel tightened wads of her skirt in her fists. Just how many years had this woman lived to have so many rolls of skin fall on her face?

Instead of a colorful long skirt, the woman was dressed in black. Lean fingers clasped rigidly on a walking stick. Those smooth hands didn't appear to know toil. How could that be, with such a weathered face? Even her voice mismatched her appearance, so youthful and spirited. Her eyes fixated on Liesel's as if the woman knew Liesel's curiosity was churning into suspicion.

"Off with you." Mother shooed Liesel away.

But she disobeyed. What did this woman want? Not food, nor did she carry any wares to sell.

"My dearest blood-born child, I fear a generation folded in your flesh must pay a consequence."

A shiver darted through her jaw. What did that mean? She stuffed her shoulder into Mother's wrap, the black one she had worn since Father died.

As though her gaze wasn't indicative enough, the woman's

long finger settled at Liesel as her head cranked to glare at Mother. "A window shall be opened. A middle-born in the brood." Gripping Liesel's chin with those fingers, the woman cast a knowing smile her way. "In time, a daughter you shall bear, my child, who will bear another."

"Time for you to go," Mother snapped.

The woman agreed with a bow, but left with her form of explanation. "You must leave space for the breath of God to enter. Else the storm will destruct."

Liesel wrapped her arms around Mother's waist. Storm?

The woman's lips curled high, and a twinkle flashed in her glittering dark eyes. Then cocking her head, she turned away.

Mother and Liesel stood, holding each other as the woman closed their front gate, the hood looming protectively around her head, her skirt swaying with ripples of grace. Rather than joining the caravan, she walked with floating steps north across the path, then headed right behind a fallow field. Their gazes lingered upon her mystique figure until it vanished.

"Mother?" Liesel asked. "Am I in trouble?"

"No. She's just a crazy wanderer, stirring up trouble." But then came Mother's dire warning. "We shall never speak of her. Nor of any of this. You shall push out of your mind such open-window nonsense and any such crazy storms. And definitely, no more Jake business. Especially those threats with that ax blade of his. Best to leave it all, everything, buried. Nothing good can come from this."

"What about Grandmother?" Liesel nodded toward the rocking chair, which happened to be eerily still. "I swear I hear it rock each night once I've bedded."

Mother's nose thrust the air upward, and with shoulders snapped and squared just like Father's used to, she avoided

Liesel's gaze and pushed her away, out of her wrap. "Hear me, child. From here on, we use this porch for storage only." She shoved the curved slats of Grandmother's rocker smack against the wall, blocking the way to the window, then locked the porch door.

And *that* was the end of that.

Or so it seemed.

# PART ONE

*If you don't have a window,
would you know a storm is coming?*

# 1

*Descendant Hanna, Canada, 1982*

"A heavy blade, it comes straight at me."

I might as well have been naked. Afraid of judgment. All this explaining felt like a confession. But the air in my chest lightened up somewhat, so I urged myself to continue.

"Slices the air like it's on some kind of mission. With some kind of wild purpose. Always a direct aim at my line of sight. The swoosh, I can't hear it. The whole business… all silent and invisible."

Imagined, all in my head? I could only wish.

"I duck and bury my face." No reason to mention how badly my hands would shake or how my shoulders could jerk about to recover from the attack. "Then nothing. There's like—nobody—just air."

"And just how often does this ax-head attack you?" The counselor leaned his forehead my way.

Finally, someone believed me.

But when he arched bushy brows and hovered his pen atop a page full of doodles in the thick notebook balanced on his lap, I wasn't so sure.

"Often enough. Sporadic," I answered anyway. "Three or four times a week. Then a month will go by, nothing." I shrugged and ogled the exit. This was a mistake.

"And just where do these plaguing manifestations happen?" He tucked his chin into his neck and fingered an ear.

Plaguing manifestations? Nope.

I gripped the armrests, squeezed their width as though they were stress balls. He thought I was making this up. He was getting paid, so shouldn't he at least indulge me?

The counselor crossed his legs, displaying shoes only loser-like, middle-aged men should wear. "Er, occurrences," he rectified.

All right, I'd play. But I had to think.

"Mostly when I'm just walking. Several times, I guess, when I'm on the bus coming home. And, once, when I was driving my mom's car. Nearly went off the road."

It was a good question, and the answer enlightened my curiosity. Kinda odd that I was always leaving one place and heading to another. The ghostly ax-head struck only when I was in transition. Did that mean anything? Why hadn't I realized that before?

He nodded, his note scribbling and foot wiggling in sync. "In other words, might your mind have been free to wander when walking, busing it, driving, perhaps?"

"I suppose." Good call. Point for him. Though the jury was still out. Was someone finally taking me seriously?

"Do you believe these are attacks to harm you?"

His gaze remained on his scrawling penmanship, ignorant of his probe's unfitting casualness.

Of course, they are. Duh! Why else would someone swing an ax at my head?

I shifted, the oversized chair feeling more like a prison. Claustrophobia was setting in. And a burn spread from where I'd rubbed my palms on the armrests. I scooted back to compose with a deep breath. "Yes, I believe they are." He'd catch on to my monotone voice. Still, he didn't look up.

Ah, crap. He didn't believe me. I could barely afford this appointment. If I called it quits now, would I get billed for less time?

"Are you disappointed in yourself, Hanna?" He paused and seemingly decided on a more direct line of inquiry. "Have you ever wanted to self-harm?"

*Now* he peered above his glasses? Self-harm! Nope again. He wasn't getting it—at all. An invisible force of some kind, a someone I couldn't see, was whacking me so hard I physically jolted. I was here because of these so-called occurrences—or whatever they were. My throat tightened and responded to a hard swallow. How to reply?

A deep stomach sigh. A few scratches at the back of my neck. Then I again eyed my coat hanging on the peg. My stocking feet planted themselves with an unmistakable firmness as I pushed away from ribbed corduroy material designed to relax its occupants.

"It's not like that," I snipped. Beads of sweat formed, thanks to the internal warmth now climbing clear to my forehead. Despite the man's kind promptings to please sit down and stay until his billing hour was up, it was no use.

He didn't get me. So much for this guy.

With it nearing 7:00 p.m., winter darkness had long fallen.

Rather than waiting, I'd save bus money and scurry the seven city blocks home. The final two, however, I'd have to be sure my wits were fully awake and on guard. My single-bedroom apartment on the edge of the city's business district meant the cost of affordability was wedged against the shadowy figures lurking in surrounding alleyways. My pace quickened.

As routine would have it, I smoothly entered the low-rise complex with a keypad code and the resultant flat buzz. Then my guarded persona scurried down a metal staircase and, with the door key lodged as a weapon between my knuckles, beelined straight to my basement apartment.

Sitting on the couch in darkness for a solid twenty minutes assured another level of safety. The best way to avoid any skulking characters outside from associating the timing of my entrance to the building with which apartment I occupied, thanks to indoor lights flicking on. Particularly important as the basement apartment's two windows had no bars, making it an easy break-in.

I prayed to God for many things, but mostly for the physical safety of my child and myself. Next, I went to the apartment one over to retrieve my twenty-month-old daughter from the babysitter. After tucking my precious girl into bed, I settled for the night on my bed, the couch. Morning would come early and, along with it, another round of demanding routines.

But thoughts wouldn't quiet.

Ugh. I tore the suffocating blankets off my chest. A rousing internal anger bolted me upright, and I sat still, blinking in the dark.

Self-harm? The nerve of that guy.

I had a reason to live, and that reason lay sleeping in the next room, the daughter I bore just after my nineteenth birthday.

I was *not* imagining things. Maybe I was a failure, but I was smart enough to know the difference between beating myself up and some phantom wanting a swing at the bridge of my nose.

Nope. That man didn't have the capability to help me.

I closed my eyes to let my overloaded mind spill.

*Parents.* I blew out the tension at the mere thought. With

my twenty-first birthday coming up, a visit was assumed. The train tickets alone will suck up my entire expendable income for the upcoming month. Although a smile lingered at the nicety. The warm and amazing aroma of Mom's kitchen coming at me once I slipped into the back door, like greeting arms hugging the soul and tugging at stomach knots.

Sadly, current realities had a way of seeping into equations. They were still angry, Mom and Dad. Old-fashioned immigrants from someplace not even on the map. "The old country," they called it. A divorced, single mother as a daughter had not been in their conservative plan book.

Mom's voice resonated, "We worked too hard for this. You've gone and ruined your whole life." I can't even repeat what Dad had to say.

After that, a full-sized elephant sucked the breathing space out of that small but cozy kitchen. Family dinners had forever changed, even though their hearts had been captured by their little granddaughter.

My arms found their way across my chest, in part due to defense but also in part to hug myself. I was always the thing no one ever wanted to talk about.

Too bad Gramma Liesel had to die. She had a special, knowing kind of smile for me. It often lingered and, somehow, allowed me to feel childlike. And we never even spoke the same language.

How I despise these nights, too worked up to sleep. No matter how trite, demons slithered into the cracks. Dozens of them, black shadows hungrily swirling inside my head, mocking my unworthiness.

Grasping my head and rocking slowly, as mightily as I could, I willed the complex emotions inside to separate. Go to their respective corners. Then I could see them, the usual suspects, for what they were.

Unrelenting anger—No one protected me. They just buried it. And forgot.

An evil grief—My innocence ripped away before I even got to my first kindergarten class.

Embarrassment—My behaviors were hard to accept sometimes, no logical reasoning for the emotions driving them.

Confusion—I was smart, yet so foolish, my confidence a pretense.

Truth be known, I hated myself. That one bothered me the most, other than when rage claimed a front seat. Those moments of darkness were terrifying.

And I *absolutely hated* when unwelcomed fragments of that warm summer afternoon years ago seemed to want to clarify. Bit by bit, the intensity built as the picture became more complete. A homemade fort in a field behind my house, made of discarded building materials from a subdivision development, my little body pressed to a dirty plank face down. Instructions to stay still. "We're not going to hurt you." Three shadows. One tall, an adult. Two shorter, kids themselves. Tree branches cut with pocketknives to smoothen them out. Poking sticks.

An involuntary shudder discharged a familiar coldness, the fragment that froze my memories—my underwear had been pulled off.

*Forget it!*

One harsh kick sent the blanket pooled at my feet flying across the shallow room. I begrudged having to pick it up. Yanking it around my shoulders, I plopped back onto the couch.

What's any of that got to do with invisible ax-heads attacking me out of thin air? "Nothing."

I was sure of it. There was no connection between my supernatural enemy and the childhood trauma I was handling.

And if my parents, who ignored it all, could lump everything under their carpet, so could I. Good thing I wore spiked heels these days—I could stomp on them anytime I wanted.

At that, a confident pillow punch, and sleep arrived.

# 2

I awoke before the alarm. Rather, an optimal idea rang instead.

A psychic! *That's* what I need.

Someone who not only believed in the invisible but also talked to them. That'd be my job today during my break at work: find a psychic in the Yellow Pages.

I dressed and whispered a thanks to God that I'd made it through another night.

Finding a psychic was easy. Plenty of coworkers were eager with recommendations. I kept mum, however, when eyebrows rose in anticipation as to why such urgency. I ignored the chatter about old wives' tales of superstition and religious no-no's. In a matter of days, I found myself sitting with rigid backbone and stretched arms across a stranger's kitchen table, my hands clasped by a woman named Clair. Middle-aged with teenage children, Clair explained herself as having natural-born skills, likened to a cross between a seer and a diviner.

Whatever. I didn't know what either meant, nor did I care. My goal was to learn more about these plaguing ax attacks. This woman could call herself whatever she wanted, as long as she produced some answers. Preferably inside an hour of billing time. After all, my rent payment was already short.

If she told me someone special was about to enter my life or to be careful with my money over the next few months, then she was fake. A young woman with moderate clothing and no wedding ring? It would be effortless to offer lines that suited. But I wouldn't bite and had already positioned my mind to be on guard.

So when Clair jerked back and pulled her hands away from the table, my defenses curled in.

"What?"

The woman's gaze bored into my face. Was her O-shaped mouth and dropped jaw suggesting our session was over?

"What?" I pleaded when the footings of her chair scratched the floor, enabling her space to get out of it. "That's it?"

"Those eyes. I don't like how he's watching you." She turned and fiddled with a dirty coffee cup on her countertop.

I was seeking a testament of reality, and I got it. I wasn't imagining these attacks. No way this woman could have known. There was, in fact, an enemy lurking.

Crud. "Who is he?!" *Dare him to show his face.*

Clair's ribs expanded with a deep suck of air. Her controlled, lean fingers nudged the pile of five-dollar bills aside, in the direction of the screen door. "You'd been warned," she uttered her final words.

I'd been warned? When? How?

Rooted to the chair, stunned, I likely appeared as a hostage. Though it was quite the opposite. Clair wanted me to leave, and I was free to take my cash payment with me.

A voice in my head interrupted. With subtlety, it took a charging lead, shooing away the fear and confusion. Calm and natural-like, it said, "Marry me."

The words soaked with an undemanding gentleness, reminiscent of a wave rolling onto a picturesque shore and melting into the countless grains of sand. This voice belonged to someone other than whoever was swinging that ax. A warm stream ran through my veins, inspiring me to absorb a renewed self-assured confidence.

I gave a hesitant glance at the pile of cash. Then I scooped it up and scampered out. No more psychics for me.

# 3

Seasons came and went. Most days normal, certainly not all. I did my best to walk through unexplainable chasms. I accepted the cruel and eager destroyer in my life, not with understanding, nor with peace, but rather with survival. I'd grown to stand firm through blade swings, not allowing my body to flinch on impact. Even so, shutting my eyes tight was unavoidable. Still, I was conquering whatever this was, whoever *he* was. And the more I stood my ground, the less he attacked. Though Clair's circling words—*"You'd been warned"*—still searched for a safe place to land.

A heads-up that an enemy wanted to strike me dead would be something I'd remember. And just who would be responsible for notifying of such an adversary?

On public transit, heading to the day care center after work, I clawed through echoes of yesterdays. Eager to have ten minutes of focus time for pensive analysis.

I pulled into memory my time as a child when, upon waking, there'd be faces, people staring down at me. Crowds of them. But, seemingly, as soon as they realized I was awake, they'd disappear. Then how about that crystal-clear scene of myself, barefoot and lost in a wheat field? It didn't seem likely that any of this had any relation to those invisible ax-head attacks. Did it?

I was amazed by how I recalled many dreams, not the regular ones. Regular ones were more like whispers that disintegrated upon rousing. For me, it was those *other* dreams, ones that came with a pounding illumination, begging me to look. Study. As if these other ones were from a different source, not a simple subconscious process. They stained my thoughts. Like a painting on my living room wall, reminding me each nightfall of a meaning I hadn't yet grasped.

And now, new evidence to behold. Reference books I'd checked out at the library said premonitions of loved ones who passed unexpectedly were often in the form of a fleeting image... or some kind of sensory detachment, an intuition. I could relate, but mine seemed more than the textbook version.

My most recent had been far more than a mere glimpse. It was an apparition. A vision of a brown coffin with a baby girl curled up at one end, a teddy on the other. Floating, literally for hours, in the middle of my living room.

At the time, I paced. Knowing intrinsically, it was not my child. Though it didn't stop me from repeatedly checking my sleeping daughter's breathing chest, ensuring its gentle rise and fall.

In that coffin, sure was sure, was someone I knew. Related. A young person. A female.

All of it, details still surreal and haunting. Smooth wood, brass handles, and only silence. The young occupant curled as in a womb. I would have had to tiptoe to see more of the box's insides. I didn't. The intrinsic notion that it wasn't my child, nor me myself, was at least something, if not selfish.

Three of my fingers covered my mouth, a warm blow of air passed through them, my exhale. I sank into the softness of the couch. It didn't do much to stop the wash of emotion. Neither did closing my eyes.

Scrambling to my knees, I asked God for answers. "Who is this? Why are you showing me this?"

As I stood, I surrendered to the urge and prayed for the wee child inside the casket. That, whoever she was, God had her safely in his arms.

The next morning, I learned of my young cousin meeting her death, because of a drunk driver. Coincidentally, the timing of the terrible accident lined up with the vision in my living room.

Weeks later, a lingering flash had appeared. An elderly man's face hung in the air. Death was at this man's doorstep, though he didn't die straightaway. A second flash of his face happened moments later. I knew the second flash suggested he had, in fact, passed through the door of death. Though I hadn't recognized his face, I knew whoever the man was, he, too, was related.

"God, allow him a safe journey home," I prayed. *Whoever he is.*

I shuddered at an image that flooded my mind: a hanging rope belonging to that so-called angel of death people talk about. The dark shadow that comes with the job to separate souls from their bodies and take them home.

Did that really happen?

Hours later, Mom called to announce that my dearly loved grandfather choked on his dinner at his long-term care home. "He didn't die right away," she continued to explain. "But several moments later, he choked a second time. It's possible too that he was stroking."

Well, they'd be together now, I reflected on the bus later. He and Gramma Liesel.

Nearly forgetting where I was, I pulled the cord. My bus stop was yards away.

With my little one in the stroller, I stopped at a play park to soak in the spring day's unusual warmth before it ended.

God must think I was special to have trusted me with this gift of a child. My daughter's little face lifted with each gentle push of the swing. And, too, by sending premonitions like that? He must be proving to me he was not only real but also in my life.

Curious. All good, but yet, curious.

# 4

Two years went by. Life changed. In those short years, I'd settled into a suburb with my new husband, who'd proven the commitment of a loving parental relationship with my young daughter. A whole family, a solid reboot. Even a new job at a bank in the central business district. And if the invisible ax attacker didn't follow, complete happiness was sure to.

Having been turned off wedding ceremonies, given my short-lived commitment in front of God at eighteen—one forced by my parents—I was hesitant to walk up to that altar and face the Divine again. Promises to the invisible were scary, especially since the invisible still had a hold on my life. So, I wholeheartedly agreed to the suggestion of City Hall's convenient legal services.

The tax-collector sort must be safer than the invisible kind, I joshed inwardly.

And family life did in fact bloom. A new son arrived, and in no time at all, I stood in front of our cul-de-sac home, waving goodbye to him as he climbed into a school bus for junior kindergarteners, my eldest already at school.

A crisp September morning, a clear blue sky, all was good. The baby I carried, my third child, stirred for its first time.

I warmed my belly with a gentle circular rub. "Well, hello," I whispered in return.

Perhaps it was pregnancy hormones, but tears gushed

unexpectedly. Accompanying emotional waves of sobs followed. An uninvited dream from the night before lingered, still vivid and fresh in my mind. That shattered blur of the past, reminding me that I deeply mourned the child within myself. Not the one I was carrying, rather my own person. That sense of being I never got to know and grew up without. The child destroyed in that fort so many years ago.

I staved off the emotions and cursed that dream. A terror, really, was what it was. A night terror. I knew it well. I'd had it countless times, each time followed by attempts to dissect it, though it brought back too many memories. The lumps under that carpet I'd shoved them all beneath churned and thumped louder than before. Fibers were tearing, my grounding wearing thin.

Nausea swirled.

Determined not to be swayed by intruding thoughts, I stuck with my plan to plant the tulip bulbs I'd purchased on the weekend. I pounded a garden fork into the hard dirt strip along the front walkway. A recent magazine article suggested tulips shouldn't be planted as single bulbs one aside the other. Rather, the new trend was in bunches. So, the hole needed to be a good size for the half dozen bulbs I had in mind.

I bludgeoned at the ground like some mechanical automation that couldn't be stopped, driven by a deep inner rage, pleased with its escape. Rapid breathing caused a dizziness I ignored. Jaw clenched, I couldn't stop hammering the earth even if I wanted to. Long-suppressed memories set my body into overload.

*Am I not worthy? No!*

Not according to that cursed dream. I was still an outsider to myself. A soul locked out from my rightful home, a protective tent that only God provides.

*I can't stand this deep isolation anymore.*

That dream allowed a supervised look through an unopened basement window, where I watched countless enemies swirling about, waving high their swords. Each fully charged and ready to slice at me should I attempt to get inside. They had taken over. Pushed me out. My own spirit not welcomed inside my own body. They stole my childhood, and now, they wanted my adulthood too.

*Curse you all. I despise this rotten, mixed-up world.*

My shoulders shook and gave way. My forehead collapsed and met the edge of the hole, now more of a pit, that I'd dug.

"God," I begged. "Please… I'm so empty. Why do I feel like this? It's like I don't know who I am. I never have."

I searched the skies for something. Anything.

"Show me, I *beg* you. Not by changing this child I carry—let them be exactly as you've willed—but through them, could you give me a glimpse? Just a hint, here and there. Something to help me see who I might've been, the child I never got to be." I pushed myself to my feet.

Feeling silly, I sulked my way back into the house and left my planting job unfinished. I muttered beneath my breath. "Because I don't know where I belong, and I'm too tired of trying to understand. It's like my soul's been lopped at, severed with chunks removed. I give up."

# 5

THE WALL CALENDAR flipped pages filled with school events, soccer practices, dance classes, and various appointments. One by one, years slipped into a pile of yesterdays. Some contributed a strengthening to my fragile confidence, while busyness offered up a false sense of belonging. The time had arrived, the inevitable, I supposed. That steady wave that rolled upon the shore had unfolded and then drifted back to sea. Taking along with it my family life and leaving in its place a crushing swell—another divorce.

I was adamant. If God had something in mind for me, a way to go, I'd keep going. "But please don't abandon me."

He was the only one I could lean on. Yet, he seemed so distant. But why? I attended church, even taught some Sunday school classes, and most of the time, did my best to live with good intentions. Perhaps best wasn't good enough. After all, well-meaning efforts didn't win out all the time.

I had to move on. Yet another foundation was needed, something to rebuild my life upon. At least this time, I wasn't in a basement apartment. Rather, I managed to find a semi with a fenced yard. My two youngest would have to share a room. My eldest, now a teenager, would be happy to hear she had the basement for herself. Nothing like our family home, but we'd make do just fine. A good place in a decent neighborhood, though its distance from the city meant grueling extra hours to my daily commute. And that was after morning drop-offs at high school for my eldest daughter, a before-school sitter for my son, and little Sadie, the baby of the family, at a preschool, a place she thoroughly enjoyed, given her outgoing social persona.

Weekends were precious.

One particular Saturday morning was quite out of the ordinary, even for someone who believed in the paranormal. All three children had been picked up the evening before for a sleepover and weekend outing. Relishing the pleasant sleep-in, I clutched a pillow for comfort. Then my senses picked up on a shift in the air.

Electric vibes wallowed, and the air thickened.

I resisted sucking in another breath. Silence. It was too quiet—not because the children were away, but because all other noise was absent. No birds chirping through the open window, no cars passing, no leaves rustling, no neighbors' dogs barking, no clock ticking, no refrigerator humming, not even the house dared its usual creaking. The dead quiet set my nerves on edge. Something was off.

Someone was here.

Behind me.

Impossible!

There was just a headboard against a wall behind my head.

Yet, I felt his presence before I could lay eyes on him.

I held a breath hostage, releasing it with controlled slowness when I could hold it no longer. Nothing I'd ever experienced prepared me for this uninvited, ghostly character in my bedroom. Still—

I could do this.

I unraveled my comforter and sidled each foot to the carpet, inching my way up to a stand. A much better position in case I need to run.

A stealthy turn to face my sponged-pink wall. A scene enveloped, swallowing up the logic of space. It wasn't faint, nor ripply. It didn't shift, nor even was it foggy. Without distortion, sharp, and unmistakable—a man, middle-aged, shabbily dressed. Some muck on dark-green and black rubber boots, worn leather suspenders, bare muscular forearms emerging from rolled-up sleeves, and a tucked-in collared shirt that had surely seen many years of wear. A wild halo of brown hair, yet his face I cannot describe. A working man of the land. His left arm hung heavily, a fist clasped around the shaft of an ax. The blade, attached with crisscross stitching, unmoving, inches from the ground.

His shoulders hunched. His right arm extended an open palm, wanting to what—clasp mine?

I coaxed my lungs to breathe, my brain to take a back seat. What did he want?

Could this be my personal enemy? That unseen stranger hoisting the ax blade. The coward, never showing his face, yet taunting me ceaselessly with the threat of death. Striking with brutal swings.

At the very least, the lack of blood on the man's blade was a good sign. But—I could be wrong. What did I know about him, or what did one expect when a ghostly stranger dropped by to visit?

A glint of light bounced from the metal edge, as if to communicate the sharp power the blade held.

I remained cautious, for his beseeching appeared raw and humble. Could this genuine pleading be nothing more than deception—a cloak-and-dagger play?

What might that man see of me, other than a tight jaw, wide

eyes, mutterings beneath shallow breath, my fingers clasping and wringing knots in my sleep shirt? Could he read my mind, feed off my emotion? Wasn't that what ghosts did?

It didn't appear I had any impact on him. If he saw I was vulnerable and afraid, wouldn't he just go for it, attack while he could? Yet, he continued with a muted and pressing appeal.

I self-declared a suggestion—leave the room. Thankfully, my legs took me up on it.

The hall washroom presented the closest escape. I locked myself inside. Splashing handfuls of cold water on my face did much to kick-start a rationalization. Just tricks. Shadows. Maybe born of past fears.

I toweled up and studied my face in the mirror. Pale. Weary. The stress of a relationship gone south, the long commute five days a week, raising three children, settling into a new normal. The wear and tear was invading my mind.

I nodded and smiled. "Get a grip, Hanna," I whispered to my image. "Of course, it's all taking a toll. You are hallucinating."

He'd be gone once I stepped back into the bedroom because he was never there in the first place.

But gone, he was not.

Not only was he still there and still pleading, but the scene had also expanded. I walked into a whole other place. Whitewashed siding hinted that a house was on his right. The ground he stood upon was flat and hard, dirt that could grow only patches of grass. The sky was a clear blue, and the day was numerous decades in the past. Why was I able to place his surroundings so easily? This plot of land he stood upon was where my ancestors once lived. The old country. Strange and well before my time. The sideboards of this old house were desperately in need of a good wash, including the single fragile glass window on the front porch. So much junk piled on the inside, surely no one lived there.

I shut my eyes, relishing a sharp exhale.

*Remember, you got this.*

I sucked in a deep breath and allowed my lungs to feel the fullness. I squared my shoulders. "What do you want?"

He carried on with his arm pulsing toward me, like I should know what he was implying. A heat rose to my cheeks because I didn't.

His eyes were so intense. I refused to look straight at them for fear I'd get fooled and drawn in, sucked into the past through some strange tunnel. Or worse, whacked by that ax-head lumbering at his side.

A buzzing sensation pulsed through my body. This time, my legs needed no instruction. I backed out, my gaze never leaving his come-hither palm. Once safely in the hall, I counted, an exit plan. Thirteen steps to the main floor, then three to the front door.

Then what? Call the police?

Huh! What would I even say? Just imagining a conversation with 9-1-1 allowed a wash of comforting humor.

Nah. *Take a breath. Just wait. He'll be gone soon.*

He had to be, right? Besides, I didn't *feel* that he wanted to hurt me.

I pushed my chest up and held my head high. *Go back in.*

After all, that was *my* room.

Nope. Still there. His arm still aching for me.

*Get a grip. No biggie. Just don't be fooled. Don't reach back.*

Oddly enough, a natural feeling overcame me. Like this visit was meant to be, as though he were sent to me. He looked like he was sorry for something. Perhaps he was asking for forgiveness?

Something he'd done in the past to an ancestor? A stretch, but hey, got anything better?

"It's okay. I forgive you," I blurted out.

But this needing, wanting pursuit of his continued. Did he not believe me?

Well, why should he? How could I mean it? I hadn't a clue what he was begging forgiveness for. Instinct hinted at a confirmation. It was something from generations ago, something before my time.

My shoulders slumped in conjunction with an exasperated depletion from my lungs.

"Well, I can't change the past," I announced.

*Whatever it was, it must have been bad for you to be here now!*

"But you've come to me for a reason."

I had a job to do, to help this man. Chin pushed up, I regained my height as an answer came calling.

"Ask God," I advised. "He is the one who knows what you did. He can forgive you."

My genuine suggestion fell on deaf ears. In fact, the arch on his back stretched forward even greater than before.

I burrowed a set of nervous toes into the carpet. My lips screwed tight, unsure if they should release my next offering. "Okay, then. If for some reason, you seek forgiveness from my family—if that is why you are here—I'll give you that. On behalf of my family… I forgive you."

*Now disappear.*

At that, he vanished. In the blink of an eye, the entire scene gone. No man, no aching arm reaching for me, no old farmhouse. The sky, the ground, *all* of it. Gone. There had been no satisfaction on his face. Nor could I sense he'd been released from any prison he may have been trapped within.

But my room was back to normal. I stepped out, took three long breaths, then stepped back in.

Nothing.

Was all that just in my head? If it weren't for the dreaded achy hollowness in the pit of my stomach, I might have just given the whole business its own special corner beneath that magical rug of denial. I wasn't ready yet—to bury it, that is. Simply too bizarre. So real. So impossible.

# 6

THERE WAS NO going back to bed that Saturday morning. My mind was trapped inside a loop of replays, rallying from one end of the spectrum to the other.

Was I special? Had I just done something amazing for my family line, a long-awaited, much-needed act of forgiveness? Was it even my business to forgive when I wasn't involved, when I didn't have a clue what damage that man had done, or when I hadn't experienced the suffering personally? How dare I be so arrogant as to think it my role to forgive?

Then again, perhaps it was personal. He was apologizing for taunting me with all those invisible ax swings. That made more sense. Then I'd be within my rights to forgive him. Still, why did he want to attack me in the first place? And *did* I truly forgive him? I should have asked him some questions. Dang, why didn't I?

I looked up, a corner where the pink-sponged wall met a yellowing ceiling. The corner I prayed to when I talked to God. "Did you see all that?" I asked him.

Figures, nothing. It'd be nice to know what he thought, though. Had I done the right thing?

Given the unspoken understanding that the man had come from an ancestor's world, a place Mom called the old country, then logic prevailed. I must call Mom if I were to get any further with the story behind all this weirdness.

Mom was a strong Christian and a believer that the divine was behind all coincidences. I accepted her faith gladly as my own, though I never told her about the invisible ax-head attacks. So, this business would be a whole new level of conversation. Desperate, I needed someone safe to talk to about this ghostly pleader.

I crossed my fingers and dialed. Were strange visitations as such a component of Christianity? It sure would have been nice if someone had warned me.

Just a single ring, Mom answered readily. Picturing her at her kitchen table still in coffee mode, I explained, swallowing shallow breaths between sentences. Hearing myself speak of the morning's events added an eerie layer of reality.

Can't say I wasn't surprised by the long pause.

But then, Mom spoke a single word. "Jake."

Wait. Had she just named my visitor?

Such matter-of-factness straddled across the telephone line, and her voice made the whole experience sound so perfectly normal. Not sure what I had expected to hear, but that wasn't it.

Seriously? She knew him to name him? I barely described him.

Anyway, let's go with it. "Jake?"

"Oma had to clean up the blood."

My turn for a pause. Oma? My gramma Liesel was involved?

Mom's weary exhale spilled through the receiver. She continued, her words came slower than normal. "In the old country. Jake struck Oma's father with an ax. She was eleven. He lived on the farm across the road."

Ah, the ax gave him away. "Did it kill him?"

"Yes, of course! Three times, he struck."

I'd never met my great-grandfather—so there was no

emotional attachment—yet the whole murder-with-an-ax-thing struck a quiet, inexplicable shock.

I sat in the thick silence, unsure where to rest my tongue. Should I side with the growing whisper that the invisible world might be more real than the one I woke up to each day? That crystal-blue sky and hard ground more tangible than my sponged-pink wall? I really needed to paint over that, by the way. Or should I take the safer route, dismiss it all with a shrug and a scoff, leaning into the comfort of disbelief?

But a deep seedling of knowing—watered with a natural curiosity and a want to analyze—planted some roots.

"Go on," I said. This was the first I'd heard of an ancestor murdered.

A great-grandfather.

By his neighbor.

With an ax.

The killer's name was Jake. That same Jake stood, in spirit form, in my bedroom, his left arm weighted down from the grip on that ax, the other outstretched and pleading. Had he been meandering in some trapped afterlife space for some, what, seventy years? Did he come to terms with his actions and was now just a misguided soul? Surely, he was seeking forgiveness.

"Why would he come to me?" The question was worth a shot, especially since Mom wasn't coming forth with much more.

"Maybe because you were named after his mother."

"What! Who would name me after a murderer's mother!"

"No, no, after your oma's father's mother, your great-great-grandmother. She never forgave Jake, used to scream at him when he walked by, called him a murderer in public. He actually called the police to have her charged, insisting she must stop harassing him."

This was confusing.

"Did the man, this Jake, *not* go to prison?" Astonished, I was. I'd just scratched the surface. There was plenty more, and I wanted the deets.

"Oh, they got him all right. But they couldn't keep him in jail long. Jake moved right back into his farmhouse. He'd gone crazy, Oma said."

"Wow. Why have you never told me this before? And why wasn't he in prison for long?"

I could only imagine my mother's thoughtful shrug at the kitchen table while she hung on to the phone. No real reason for not telling me this before, yet perhaps no real reason *to* tell it. "Oma warned me not to talk about it. She wasn't supposed to, either. And neither should you. So keep it to yourself."

"Come on." I ground my teeth. "I need to know."

"He warned her."

"Who warned her? What do you mean?"

"Said she'd better keep quiet and learn to sleep with one eye open. He wasn't going to rest until he axed her entire family. He wouldn't stop till they were all gone, he'd promised."

Okay, great. Perhaps I shouldn't have forgiven him. "I want to hear more."

"I've said enough. You needn't know any more."

"Maybe he's sorry now," I offered up.

"Are you sure it was Jake?"

Seriously? *She* was asking *me* that? "Who else would it be?"

A stillness hung, weighing down the telephone lines across our two cities. She obviously doubted his regret.

"I gotta make the bed," she announced.

"Okay."

Not fair. Of course, she didn't want to talk about this anymore. Now, she'd stew about it, wishing she hadn't told me anything. There was more to this story, but I'd have to pick the right time to get the rest of it.

That man had carried an unmistakable air of pleading. He was desperate. He needed to be freed. And wasn't that what God wanted me to do? Forgive him? Right or wrong, so I had.

Still, had I somehow allowed interference and betrayed my ancestors?

Stirring my third cup of coffee later that morning, tearing apart possible solutions, I stilled at an enlightened line of thought. I'd heard of emotional trauma being channeled by women to future generations, particularly to granddaughters.

Perhaps this was biological, with some kind of scientific explanation that only those studying it could understand. Had I inherited a manifestation that ultimately presented itself? A phantom imprint in the brain. An echo of fear passed through generations.

If Gramma Liesel's father was killed with such brutality on his front porch, she was certain to have been present, perhaps even a firsthand witness. What horror! Had time needed to pass until a generation with less attached connection existed, a family member open and willing to free the descendant's line of imprisoned unforgiveness?

I spent the afternoon and evening flipping through the Bible. God surely must have something to say about this. Perhaps unforgiveness was some kind of spiritual stronghold that must be broken. Like the bitter root noted in Hebrews 12:15 that grows to cause trouble to others. Forgiveness was nonnegotiable if one wanted spiritual freedom, according to Matthew 6:14. It wasn't a far stretch that unforgiveness could have generational consequences, and one way to break the cycle and bring about healing to the whole line would, of course, be through the act of forgiveness.

By the time I settled into bed for the evening, I was nearly satisfied with settled thoughts of Jake and my ancestors and even what God was possibly attempting to accomplish. Though Mom's final question as to the certainty of identification was disturbing. It would be ridiculous *not* to presume this man was that Jake, the man Mom herself spoke of, the ax murderer from decades gone by. And let's not forget, the likely one behind all those ax-head attacks on me.

But worse, if the act of unforgiveness was so powerful to cause such a spiritual disruption, then I faced the rubbing challenge to forgive those who violated my body and stole my innocence at such a young and tender age. Instead of forgiving, I'd kept from drowning, there'd be so many others with considerably more dreadful stories to tell.

A familiar harshness clenched my jaw. Still, not fair. If I were to forgive them, then I'd be forced to deal with the reality that it *actually* happened.

I wasn't ready for that. Not yet.

# 7

IN THE NEXT five years, the absurd story of Jake, that wandering soul from the afterlife seeking forgiveness, barely surfaced after the man's visitation. Except for perhaps two or three times, when plenty of laughs and a few drinks with friends presented a safe and intriguing environment to share a unique and wild tale. Then, like a diary with villainous entries, he'd be stuffed back under that carpet, which at times gave my walk in life an uncomfortable stumble.

I married once again, this time vowing it would be forever. As a little girl, I'd never imagined such marital turmoil would mark my path. As happiness and stability increased in my heart and home, so seemed a watchful eye, sending more and more messages—visions that spoke without words, warnings folded into dreams, even a voice that came not from this world. To me, it felt like my soul was unveiling secret truths, the unseen kind. Some harmless, some concerning. I made valiant attempts to tear each apart and analyze. This other world was not finished with me yet, and I needed to know why. A few of the more recent visions—

A cold metal gurney in a space fully adorned with flowers, the night before the news of Lady Diana's tragic death—a simple premonition. No biggie. Plenty of folks around the globe must've had something similar.

Another time, there I was, at the tail end of a long and narrow space, no ceiling, no walls, but like an infinite classroom, rows of ornate gold pedestals, each with an open book atop it. Floating pens with eyes scribbled, some swift with frenzied speed, others meditatively slow. No explanation was needed. This, a sacred space, was where spoken words and silent thoughts were being recorded. A book bestowed to each mortal in passage, a living quill assigned to scribe. As Psalm 139:1–2, Hebrews 4:12–13, and Proverbs 15:11 declare, he hears and knows our innermost thoughts. All of it. All the time.

That one tugged at me—my first glimpse of heaven—a teaching of wisdom. A reminder to heed one's thoughts and caution one's tongue.

Then there was a time of scolding—

As I climbed into bed, quiet words of warning pressed into my ears. "Mind your ego. It's obvious."

The message carried the warmth of a parent's love, though unmistakably underscored with a dreadful action, should I choose not to listen.

But ego? Me? I suffer from nonconfidence. I was a follower, not a leader. I shrank from conflict.

Yet, there it was, some kind of warning. Perhaps the warning that psychic Clair so long ago talked about? Timing from that other world didn't seem to line up with this one. Of course, then again, time as we know it likely didn't exist there.

For days, I self-examined my actions. How was it possible to exist in a society where personal achievement was greatly honored and self-promotion was almost a must and often encouraged? Much more, it was rewarded.

Ego was closely associated with pride. God hated pride.

Deflated, I vowed to remember these whispered words, this rebuking of sorts.

One afternoon, when I wanted nothing more than a nap, which my busy schedule couldn't possibly allow, an entire scene appeared. After watching, I cast it away—

Just as ordinary as anything, Jesus himself came strolling toward me through where one might expect, a brilliant pasture of greens, wearing also what one might expect, a flowing white robe. Blue sky behind him, a knee-high white fence between us. A rather large and transparent hand appeared from the blue space above him, pointing a finger at me. God. It was the hand of God. Neither was it accusing nor harsh. Still, it was rather deliberate. The finger counted the bodies standing to my right. One. Two. Then three. At the third, the hand rotated, palm upward, and pulled in its fingers. Come, it motioned. And pop, the third body on my right, a little girl all dressed in white, left my side with zero hesitation and ran to Jesus, who was waiting on his side of the fence. He picked her up and over. She hugged him fiercely. They turned without as much as a glance my way. As they strolled back, hand in hand, the little girl skipping, to wherever Jesus had come, the scene disappeared. It was all so natural. So telling.

But, no, it couldn't be. God didn't mean he was going to take my third child from me. Did he? Sadie, my bubbly, spirited child? She was barely ten years old. He wouldn't do that. Would he? And how quickly she left when he called!

Far too disturbing. I shoved this one under the carpet. I cursed my mind, these visions. *Don't be ridiculous. God doesn't do stuff like that!*

# PART TWO

*One must keep a window open
to catch the breeze that binds.*

# 8

The years passed with barely a blink. Much changed. We all grew. My oldest daughter was readying for her special day, an outdoor wedding in the countryside. My son, working steadily on his music talents. Sadie in her element, her third year of high school and surely the most organized socialite to walk the halls. My husband's business booming. Our families—his two children and my three—beginning to jell. As for me, I had gone back to school and snatched an MBA, although "snatched" hardly describes the sacrificed time and energy involved. The 2007 calendar highlighted the coming Sunday, Father's Day.

That finger-pointing, one-two-three vision was long expunged from my head. Anything I'd heard over the years from any sermon, minister, pastor, or faith magazine was clear: God didn't look to harm us. He wanted nothing but blessings to come our way.

So I'd convinced myself my mind was playing tricks and the inner forge had gone too far. As the power of that scene faded, I wearied myself from the business of piecing together fragmented dreams and visions. Including that arcane visitation, heaven forbid. I stopped offering up the energy to analyze, much less entertain, anything nonlogical, even though they still came in plenty.

But then, it hit. The storm of all storms without warning. I was forced to pay attention.

That morning, all had been doggedly normal. I'd dressed to prepare for a series of business meetings, all while dreading that long early morning commute into the financial district and aching for retirement to break free miraculously from its two-decades-away grip. There was much on my mind.

Then, with a jolt, only one thing—

A sheath of blackness slammed, escaping my nose by mere inches. I swallowed hard, and my neatly folded suit jacket slipped from my elbow. My body went too rigid to move, paralyzed by this heavy veil that dropped with such urgency from above. It felt deliberate, much like the fell of a hatchet. If it weren't for the single sliver of brilliant light that traced along the seam of the floor, I would have been in total darkness. I was certain this was it. The final curtain had descended.

Today was the day I would die.

What else could God mean by this?

For certain, the end was imminent. Of course, his timing isn't ours. Perhaps it wasn't today. Perhaps it was a matter of days or even weeks. Nevertheless, no question, it was a done deal.

I surprised even myself. "Okay, God, I am ready," I whispered. "But you've got to help them through this."

I ached for my family who'd suffer such a blow as the untimely death of their mother and wife.

"If this is your will, God, then… then"—a deep breath pushed the rest out—"so be it." I straightened my spine and let the words soak in.

Maybe, since that solid veil hadn't met the floor, it meant I'd have a slight chance to say goodbye.

How was it I was so strangely calm, so detached?

Maybe this would sink in later.

Nothing happened along the highway drive into work. I

found myself watching the road with extra caution and stilling as each transport flew past. It would likely be a traffic accident. Might another car's tire blow and a series of chaotic maneuvers follow? A snort of lunacy escaped when I parked safely in my usual overpriced parking lot. "Too bad, I must put in another day at work." A sick sense of humor, I admit.

During the long day of meeting after meeting, I had to excuse myself for washroom visits a number of times. A heavy gnawing chewed away at my inner organs, ripping and tearing as a vulture would to roadkill. Except I wasn't dead. Not yet, anyway.

A dark sadness, a feeling I'd not experienced before, wrapped long, ugly fingers around my neck. I heard my voice explaining away a bout of tears to cohorts, "Darn cold coming on. My eyes are runny." I was struggling to hold a pen and repeatedly wiped sweat off my hands along my skirt. Grim thoughts of my life coming to an end swallowed me into a deep darkness.

Was I truly okay with this? Had I accomplished what God needed me to do? Somehow, there was a purpose he'd given me, and somehow, I'd completed it. Right? I could only wish. I doubted I'd ever found my true purpose. Not for lack of trying.

Finally, an end to the workday, a ceasing of mouths snapping in my direction, minds vying for attention, and cold stares judging. I need to be alone in my thoughts, just me and my commute home. The radio off, and only deep breaths to accompany the stirrings of confusion. What I experienced in my room this morning was dreadfully real.

Dozens of other commuters fought for priority positioning on highway ramps. Rather than challenge, I let them all through, an accompanying chorus of car honks behind me. I hadn't gotten far when my mobile rang. I introduced myself, business protocol and all.

The caller seemed awkward. A private clinic. I had taken Sadie, now seventeen, for an X-ray the day before, or was it the day before that? She'd been complaining about pain and stiffness for a couple of weeks after she'd taken up tennis. With her being more of a shopper than a sporty girl, her shoulder injury hadn't surprised me, yet it wasn't going away.

A dire urging flowed from the speaker, suggesting I follow up with the doctor as soon as possible. "Tomorrow morning. Go there," he said.

After pressing him, I took the liberty of reading between the lines.

He named several reasons her shoulder could be so painful, then added, "However, one possible explanation for Sadie's discomfort is serious. In fact, it could be a type of sarcoma."

"Sarcoma—that's cancer, right?"

While he remained evasive, I knew in an instant. My guess was not simply a possibility: it was a sure thing.

This changed everything. "No way, God. You cannot take my daughter!"

A violent wave had crashed onto my shore, a place where I'd finally been able to stand firm with both feet. The angry waters loosened my footing and dragged me in pieces back out to sea. I struggled to stay afloat.

*Seriously, God! Is this how you work?*

# 9

"Cisplatin," "doxorubicin," and "methotrexate"—all were new and critical utterances to spring off my tongue. Sadie's upper arm bone was growing bone. A huge, hard mass with accelerated growth thanks to its own private network of sneaky blood veins. They called it osteosarcoma.

Limb-salvage surgery to her right arm would eventually happen, but anything to do with tomorrow was just a fog. Preserving the here and now of the present became my daily mandate. Although our adopted outlook bowed as a rainbow, sunlight shone through the rain and the promise of a safe landing. This experience would simply be one year of Sadie's life when she'd be planted anew—to a landing spot where she'd be stronger in faith and have grown the character and will for her God-given purpose in life. She was brilliant, took one day at a time, and not only carried this outlook but also preached it to her friends. On top of it all, she remained true to her personal brand, a natural-born giggler.

I worked at home and at the hospital as much as possible and took chunks of time off here and there when needed. Sadie relished the love and support of her family—siblings, parents, and friends often at her side or just a text away.

I summoned those scribbling pens atop those books of life resting on pedestals. The notion of my thoughts and words being recorded went far to dissolve my anger. Surely, God was with us and not against us. He had his reasons, I supposed. Each night, I kneeled at my bedside, confident he had us in his hands. "Don't let us go," I pleaded. Fear still loved to travel up and down my veins like a rigid north-south urban subway. I needed to be extra careful not to upset him. Just how thick was my book on that pedestal, and how many gold-rimmed pages were in Sadie's?

*Please, God, let there be countless more to come for hers!*

I even apologized to him, needing to cover a plaguing possibility. Was this my punishment for not forgiving?

*I've tried, God. You know that.*

They took my childhood from me.

*You of all should understand.*

This tall and looming black shadow, an evil lurker without a name. I didn't even know who he was to forgive. As far as I was concerned, he could stay that way. Faceless. Nameless. The other two, just kids. Barely three years older than I was. I talked myself into forgiving them. That had to count for something. After all, they were victims too, made to watch and partake.

I paused.

Was this some kind of test?

That seemed more like the God I'd read about. Countless Scriptures gave testament. Tests were purposeful, meant to reveal what one is harboring.

Well, that confirmed it, as far as I could figure.

If, in this storm, God wanted to break open my heart to see what he'd find, then I'd better be sure to show him I wasn't one to lose hope, despite the severity and threatening odds of Sadie's cancerous disease.

But what if he saw the unforgiveness?

At a shiver, I looked around for my sweater.

And if God's heavenly servants were always listening, recording all thoughts and sentences, then, well, he'd find out. I couldn't have that. Sadie must have every possible chance.

That evening, I kneeled at my bedside. Anxious and eager to say the words aloud.

"God, I forgive all those who caused such harm in my early years." I paused.

A great sadness of remembrance fell into my heart, weighing it down. *At least I will do my best to try.*

All I could think of were the years stolen from me.

So many moments, classroom days from kindergarten to college, when fingers of a dark shame stroked my hair as if it cared, yet it mocked. My value could never be. Forever the unwanted. The very last to be chosen for absolutely anything.

I hated that feeling and, by now, knew it was all an evil lie. Nevertheless, it was the lie I grew up with, and its remnants still attacked a charge at me now and again.

"I'll focus on hope, God. Your hope, the gift you provided. I accept it with thanks."

I pushed up to my feet.

*Hope* was one thing.

*Trust* was quite another.

How did one rebuild an instinct to trust? It seemed like God asked the impossible of me. Didn't he know there were so many times when giving up would have been easier?

Not long after, I began the practice of daily journaling, most notably to jot down vivid dreams and clips of visions that seemed to announce something I needed to know. I started to pay close attention again. The sense of profoundness, the specificity of details, and the images that remained. I dismissed anything that disintegrated into fog and thin air quickly, my mind unable to snatch anything concrete. Many times, I found myself in the dream. I'd be watching myself witness something, another being always near, standing behind me. Sometimes quietly and other times only speaking when needed—

I was in this dream. A younger version that is, perhaps in my early twenties. Barefoot and dressed in loose and flowing whiteness, I strolled toward a wide set of stairs.

At first, that was all I could see: those wide steps. They were firm, much like concrete in steel grips, and appeared suitable to withstand the outdoor elements for those times when nature chose to lack mercy. Seven risers in all, its daring ascent led to a sacred altar. Rectangular in shape, with marble-smooth white sides.

Flames poked from the top. Blue and orange hues flickered in harmony, dancing to a tune I was forbidden to hear.

Following instructions from someone, not sure who, I climbed each step. No hesitation. I even admired my posture, how tall and graceful it was. Yet I knew that heart inside my chest cavity was pounding and preferred to turn and run. But my legs kept steady and strong. My breath was arrested as the inevitable next instruction came without as much as a whisper.

I was prompted to hike myself up and onto the altar. To lie flat and still among those flames.

Mechanically, I obeyed.

Chest high, the structure offered little to grip other than the altar's edge. Oddly, it was cool to the touch.

Forearm muscles hauled me up. Once one leg had swung over, the rest followed.

I stretched out and laid my arms at my sides. I fit perfectly, as though the fiery pedestal had been custom-made.

Why bother to get someone comfortable just before incinerating them to ashes?

I closed my eyes and prayed for it to be over. *Quickly, please. Just relax.*

My job was clear: to surrender. Still, I wasn't sure how.

I waited and waited. Finally, I opened my eyes.

There was no pain. Nor even heat, though flames encircled and loomed high, burning hungrily.

How was it I couldn't feel anything? Was I suddenly flame-resistant?

The real-life me awoke in a panic. Sweat beaded up on my forehead, evidence of a primary response—fear. I pushed my back against my headboard, the anticipated sunrise just moments away, and asked God, "Am I to be some kind of sacrifice?"

It didn't feel right. Sadie's diagnosis threatened *her* life, not mine. As a mother, I wished to change places with her. Maybe this was simply a psychological thing. Or maybe not.

"God, are you testing me? Is that what this is all about?"

He was playing a game. I wasn't sure I liked it much.

# 10

THE DAY ARRIVED for Sadie's surgery. The diseased humerus bone would be removed and replaced with a prosthetic implant. Nerves and blood vessels would be preserved as much as possible, muscles and tendons to be reattached to the prosthesis.

It was a long day. One that marked the beginning of a new phase in Sadie's medical journey. Next, we'd face healing for bone and marrow, nerves and muscles, and wound care for eighteen inches of stitched-up arm flesh that had been cut wide apart.

A new regime of pain management for Sadie, and a new kind of ache for me. A horror of guilt, so irrational. Could I have prevented my child from this? Any parent might cross barriers with such thoughts. A burning sense of protective longing could do nothing to fix my child's body or to ease the gnawing torment of seething pain. A mother's care replaced with oxycodone.

Eventually, we'd begin chemotherapy treatment again.

It is said that anxiety and fear can go a long way to conjure up an overactive mind. These tiring months found me heady with spirituality. Obsessed with life and death, or rather, life-death-then-life again.

But something was going on in the heavens. Something was forcing this dilemma into our lives on earth. I fixated on the thought. And I had no one who could understand this, no one to talk to.

I argued internally—reassuring myself I hadn't lost my marbles. I was simply overthinking things, right? And overthinking led to imagining.

Contrary to the simple explanations, dreams continued with increased frequency and intensity. Images symbolic and profound and quite often helpful—

I was falling, though not sure into what. That part of the dream remained vague.

Then the scene morphed and sharpened. A space opened up by my feet on the floor. I sat on a plain stacking chair, center stage, peeking into the horizontal window below. An entire orchestra was playing. They played a sad tune, and tears formed. They played an ominous chord, and I shivered. They played happy music from my childhood, and I recalled skipping with my friends.

It was blatantly obvious. The music they played determined my emotions, even triggered memories! The people in the orchestra were "playing" me with "all strings attached," so to speak, in order to provoke me into an emotion of their will.

Each musician focused on a faceless conductor and was rewarded for how well they played. Getting into that orchestra was considered an honor. But this particular conductor was evil.

I don't know if the players knew how terrible their role in the vile plan was. Their ability to play music was exceptional and beautiful, but the overall purpose of their harmony held deceiving and despicable impacts.

Over the next months, I appreciated this dream, calling upon it when my heart ran wild with emotion. "Don't get played," I'd charge myself. That orchestra was an effective and organized mechanism to move me into a state of great worry and fear whenever it pleased.

In those moments, I thanked God for the caution and begged him to be with Sadie at all times. Then I'd take a time-out to consider and release blocks of emotions that interrupted my faith. Pen and notebook handy, I fell into an image, not one from a vision or dream, but rather from my inner sense, a need for survival. The depiction of my storm took on a life of its own—

A tornado. We were smack in the center, Sadie and I. Ferocious winds howled, circling with twisting daggers hidden in the swirling debris. Deafening noise surrounded, but inside, a still chord of intangible solace. We simply had to hold onto it. This storm demanded respect. If we shifted, left or right, forward or back, such disobedience meant evil was entitled to take a cutting. Below us, the safe space narrowed into a black churn, eager to grind our souls into bits. Above us, the sky was ample with crystal-blue hues. Wide with hope and future.

This storm was going to take us somewhere, away from the ground we stood upon. I just knew it. We must stay centered with the lifeline God provided and always look up. Trust him. Have faith. He would carry us. We just had to remain still, let him do the navigating.

The image made me feel safe. Lean into God. I just had to remember that.

Light beamed through the sunroom window. I settled back to let its warmth soak into my persona.

*So, God, just where are you moving us to?*

Huh, one of those dreams I'd had, back in the year of that Jake visitation, poured its way into my thoughts with vivid clarity. At the time, I chalked it up to all those inner battles that reminded me I'd been sidetracked at life's early stages. Hinting that now, I was securely on the wrong path, not a path meant for me. But what did one do with that notion? It wasn't like the clock of time could be turned back. So I tucked it away, beneath that carpet—

I was climbing a mountain and nearing the top third. I stopped to rest and look around, the scenery incredible with widespread peace and freedom. Satisfied with how far I'd come, I remained aware I still had quite the climb to the summit. The future bit would be more treacherous and unforgiving, but this was my personal journey in life. Everyone had a mountain to climb.

Then the scene changed. Another solid mountain stood gloriously tall beside mine, blocking my view. Why hadn't I seen it before? As I searched for its peak, realization uprooted me. My footing weakened, and a silent voice inside screamed with horror at the mistake I'd made.

I am supposed to be on *that* mountain!

If only I had wings, I could fly across the sky to that other mountain, get to where I needed to be. But I didn't. Rather, I awoke in disoriented dread, unsure what to do with the nauseating knot in my stomach. Descend a mountain and start all over? How could I connect with such a thought? Even in the parabolic image to life itself, one does not become a newborn to start afresh. Didn't a biblical character ask something similar?

Perhaps God was moving me to the right mountain. Perhaps that was what he intended to do with this storm he clothed me in. Whisk me across the sky inside a hidden storm, so I might land on the mountain I was supposed to be climbing in the first place. Was I taking Sadie with me? Were we traveling together in this? Her storm was led by the physical, while mine felt led by the spiritual.

At least the thought served an awarding chuckle. My

ingenuity to connect dreams and conjured images was helpful indeed.

Though, if this was what God wanted, well then, there was more to come. And I'd need to hang on tight.

## 11

**We were nearing** the end of the post-surgery treatment regimen. Months had gone by before it came to an abrupt end.

Sadie had been wearing from the aggressive rounds of chemotherapy infusions. So, when a ghastly case of peripheral neuropathy occurred, causing her fingers to stiffen temporarily into clawlike formations and her doctor decreed "No more infusions for you," she was relieved.

Her body was unable to carry on. We were discharged within the hour of fingers returning to normal and on the highway heading home.

With my head in a spin, I struggled to focus on the traffic. The loss of Sadie's physical control had been terrifying, and the abruptness of being released prematurely stirred something deep and cold inside.

But Sadie was elated. As far as she was concerned, she was finished with treatments and nothing but pure golden days lay ahead. Rest and recovery and getting on with life were up next on her agenda. Deep breaths and nonstop chatter all the way home. "Let's have a big party, Mama!"

Somehow, the label Remission swirled about our tiny corner of the world, even though nary a doctor or medical practitioner uttered the word. It defined her, and she'd gobbled it up as if it were warm chocolate lava cake, complete with caramel drizzle and ice cream. And so, celebrate with her, we did.

But the sideways nod of the surgeon's head when he claimed they got "most of it" during surgery and then the recent rejection of postoperative treatment left me with inescapable dread. I tried to bury it, though my insides recoiled. Too much was left unspoken. "Most of it" meant "not all of it." That evil gnawing of growth was still in her body. So we were playing a wait-and-see game. And the challenge of treatment had gone up more than a notch.

With each drink of air, my heart replenished itself with God's promise—faith. *Sadie's cancer shall not return.*

I still hadn't mastered trust. Wouldn't he cut me some slack on that? So, too, with each bite of that celebration cake, I must trust him. Watching Sadie enjoying her friends—her happy eagerness to share her story and her sense of accomplishment—brought much-needed warmth and internal satisfaction. More than any cake ever could.

*He's got this. He has to.*

No denying it. Our house had been turned upside down and shaken hard. Our next job was to clean up the broken pieces, put away the chaos, and reintroduce normality to our living space. Only, now, a new resting place was required—an inner haven fully protected with God's wisdom. And *that* was an urgent need.

The so-called remission we all bought into was short-lived. A matter of weeks.

We were scattering about to prepare for a happy Friday evening out, Sadie with her friends, my husband and I with ours. Sadie inspected my outfit. That full hands-on-hips and crooked nod of hers. "Nope, Mother. Not *that!*"

I smirked. "You must be serious about my fashion choice to call me mother."

She just rolled her eyes.

But it was true. When we were alone, I was always Mama. I relished the quiet, childlike manner. When her brother was around, she matched his use of Mother Dear, and when all the family was present, Sadie joined in with "Hey, Big Mama."

As she provided suggestions as to how I might stay on point with the latest trends, I reveled in the joy of her spark. Her zest for life was pure—love and laughter, family and friends.

No one heard the phone ring. Or perhaps it was some kind of telepathy, an alarm that something was wrong and, if we avoided it, it would go away. Besides, if it were important, they'd call back.

Upon returning from our dinner out, I listened to the message. One of Sadie's doctors. Rare it was for them to call directly. And on a Friday evening, no less. His recorded words were deafening—no, *sickening*. Witness I became to a trembling hand—mine—hovering over the machine, daring to press Delete.

Still, the speaker crackled along: "More cancer... New tumors... Lungs... Shoulder... Monday appointment, right after the weekend. Ten o'clock. Blood work first."

The devil was dancing, eagerly spreading his seed. Sadie's routine scan results were proof of it.

Nauseated at the very idea of preparing for another battle round, I shook my fist at God. "Are you *not* protecting us?"

He'd led us in close, then let a hammer fall. No, not a hammer, a hatchet. A hatchet blade as wide as a room, the one that fell inches from my nose last year when Sadie was diagnosed. And darn it all, curse that Jake guy and his stupid ax too.

*To all of you, hiding in the invisible, I hate you all!*

I don't know why that Jake memory invaded my mind at that

moment. Somehow, he'd forced his way in, flipping all kinds of switches, provoking reminders of betrayal and deception.

How was I supposed to tell Sadie?

God would have no choice but to hear me, day in and day out. Ceaseless begging. *Please, just heal her.*

Forty-eight hours. That was the agreed-upon limit Sadie and I allowed ourselves to grieve, stomp, and curse after the discouraging news. I hoped God had forgiven my rageful outburst directed straight at him in less time than that.

"God, you *know* how much she loves you, and you know I love you too. Why are you letting this happen? We could testify for you, if only you'd heal her, show the world what you can do. We can't fight this battle. *You* must. We all surrender! Isn't that what you want?"

*Hadn't that sacrificial altar with no threat to its flames meant I should trust you? I wouldn't be harmed through this? I shouldn't worry? That all would be okay?*

"Well, God, I *am* hurting. The flames are, in fact, burning. Can't you see what is happening to Sadie? All is *not* okay!"

Over the next days, my begging must have worn him down. Another message came, rather a command. Loud and clear. But it wasn't what I expected to hear—

I was responding to a friend's encouraging email, and as I tapped out my appreciation on the keyboard, a single word exploded into my ear, commanding my complete attention.

"STOP."

There was no mistaking it. The echoing voice of God. *My* God. The very one I leaned into for comfort, for guidance. The man about the house to fix things, all things spiritual, that is.

My muscles seized, frozen by shock at the directive tone. My fingertips remained in position, midsentence, hovering over the keyboard.

Stop? There was no denying the instruction.

My eyebrows dared the first move, my gaze scouring the ceiling. Any scenes unfolding? Might some angelic guard be standing behind me? Sent to discipline? Nerves on high alert, I scanned the room. No hallowed figure or divine image to be seen, just Sadie, out cold in one of her frequent twenty-minute, post-pain-medication naps. I doubted any divine being would hide behind her oversized recliner. No one but me and Sadie in the room—unless you counted the cutting chill in the air as a presence.

"Did I hear you right?" I had to ask, though there'd been no doubt.

God had directed me to stop. And I knew instinctively what for. All the incessant begging for a complete healing. My let-Sadie-live-for-Pete's-sake attitude.

My mouth gaped wide as my hands splayed upward with a questioning gesture. Where had I made that wrong turn? Even this new foundation I'd been building was already starting to crumble.

Perhaps my interpretations were way off base. Because, let's face it, God would never tell me to stop praying for healing. Right?

Sure, I'd been angry with him, but try as I might to steady myself with scriptural reason, God's ways could be the extreme from ours. Still, head heavy in my hands and with long blank stares at the floorboards, I strained my chest well beyond the point of weeping.

God was trying to break me. "Go ahead. Smash me to bits. I probably deserve it."

I was no expert in Bible verses, though specific ones stuck in my mind through the years, particularly the odd, unusual ones. Like the command of Jesus to Peter in Matthew 16:23: "Get behind me, Satan! You are a stumbling block to me; you do not have in mind the concerns of God, but merely human concerns."

All Peter wanted to do was pray away the suffering that Jesus was about to face.

The command must have been a shock to Peter, as God's command to stop the pleas was to me. Was I in the way of God's pursuit of some greater goodness? A stumbling block to be more precise.

Ridiculous! Surely, Sadie's suffering was *not* God's plan.

The vortex beneath my feet swirled in mockery. Velvety, seductive music tempted me into the tornado's destructive funnel. If I wanted to stay afloat in the safety of the storm's core, I'd have to keep that neck and head of mine straining toward the sky above. Trust God knew what he was doing with that Stop command. Up the ante of my faith.

Especially since I sensed it, the wrathful black wind surrounding me was gearing up, preparing for launch. I was departing from my mountain. Whatever trust I'd built, I'd have to rely on. Those were my new wings. There would be no going back after takeoff.

## 12

**Battle Round 2** was, indeed, tougher.

Faith and trust had to work together: one was not good enough without the other.

Believing God existed came easily, especially since I believed I'd experienced the truth of his existence from my early days. The unseen, as far as I was concerned, had shown its face. So, faith was natural, a given.

Trust, not so natural. That had been harder. It called for full reliance. How could I trust him fully, when he hadn't protected my childhood innocence then, nor my child's health now? My relationship with him wasn't exactly grounded in the I-saved-you-from-harm kind of deal.

I believed God *could* heal Sadie. Whether he *would* or not was another thing.

All I could do was hope.

In my journal, I captured an upsetting vision. I was sitting on the outside window ledge of a skyscraper, battling the intense apprehension of a fall, given that the ledge was slowly shrinking in size. Was God just a hungry lion wanting my blood splattered on the cement pavement far below, my organs exposed for circling vultures? Well, if he did, it was a matter of time before that was what he got.

Yet, I contemplated that high-rise building. Strong authority, representing a mighty power, safe and bright on the inside.

There I sat, perched outside on a narrowing ledge, exposed to whatever nature conjured up. People inside could see me, yet because of the commercially sealed window, they could do nothing.

I was left to cope with the elements and balance on my buttocks as best as I could. Was that window truly unopenable? Had I checked, might I have gotten inside? And aside from a devastating plunge that would surely seal my fate, what was that uneasy sense of goading in the air?

Ah, a similarity amused me. That childhood dream. Or rather, night terror. For so many years, it repeated. It was likely one of the first lumps I shoved under that carpet of mine. Like a taunting meant to teach, simple in some respects, though I just wasn't getting it. How did one resolve such windowpane dilemmas?

A barefoot child was I, no more than five years of age. Locked outside my house in the pitch dark of night. A streetlamp in the distance shone, but its light didn't reach where I stood. Of course, it wouldn't; it was man-made, a mere imitation of true light. I crouched near the east-facing basement window where a presence, the True Light, stood behind and encouraged me to look inside. So I did.

All those bearded men, at least forty of them, their ancient flowing garbs swirling with choreographed command, blocked me from entering my rightful home.

If it weren't for the window, would I have known the realm of a loving home, a safe environment, a place that harbored wisdom with steadfast strength even existed? Might I have been content to remain as an outsider had I not had a glimpse? Rather, instead, I would make the dark exterior my abode and accept the disappearing ledge to be fate, knowing that death would inevitably come.

What chance did I have to change the outcome?

It wasn't enough to be a locked-out survivor—enemies on the inside, death on the outside—I had to be high up on the wrong mountain. Go figure.

# 13

IN THE EARLY hours of a new sunrise, God showed me a map. A triangular mass of land with narrow waterways on either side. The outline resembled a dagger pointing downward.

For heaven's sake, where on earth was *that?*

I shuffled my pillows, unfolded at the waist, and pushed myself to a sitting position, fully awake and eager to survey this blueprint of sorts. No need to turn on the bedside lamp. The vision was distinctive and clear, as usual.

No expert on the geographical markings of ancient lands, particularly anything that might have been considered holy, I was grateful for the knowledge embedded in the simple outline of mountains, waters, and travel ways.

And God was on the move. Or he was telling me I was.

His index finger started at the northeast corner. As the translucent tendril moved southbound, it paused halfway down the edge. A line drawing followed, measuring how far I'd come, as if that was where I stood on the map. Notably, a mountainous range with jagged rocks and desert lay to the west of the pause. Wasn't that where the Israelites wandered about for all those years, doubting God?

His finger stayed put in that place of rest. My brain hurt, desperate for a greater understanding.

*What are you showing me?*

A line sketched with dots darted straight west, then across a narrow body of water and settled somewhere on Egypt's mainland. The dotted line disappeared, as though it had been the original route God had in mind for me, but now he was deciding to change things up.

*Where to now?*

His finger was on the move again. Further southbound and around the bottom of the peninsula, a terrain that appeared rough and impossible to travel by foot, then north up the west side of the triangle. It stopped halfway, then popped over that waterway again and landed in Egypt, at the same spot.

So, we were taking the long route. Was that what this second battle round was all about? Inevitably, we were going to end up at the same place. Somewhere in Egypt.

But was that a safe place to land? From things I'd read, I believed Egypt to be a temporary place of safety. It wasn't home per se, rather a place to stay hidden, all while being provided for.

I slid back under my duvet, pulling it high around my neck. It didn't make a lot of sense. In fact, it was rather discouraging. From where would the energy come to take the long route? I shoved a pillow around my ears as if that would quiet the confusion of the map hanging above my head. Then I slipped back into a state of slumber.

Sadie's care requirements were considerably different in this second leg of the journey. No longer those three or four overnight chemo stays. Instead, an increase in the number of driving days on the highway into the heart of the city center for scans, doctor visits, chemo infusions, blood work, then fighting rush-hour traffic home. More than a few times, we pulled over somewhere halfway home so Sadie could vomit. That, too, became routine. Local visits to the emergency hospital due to high fevers also increased. As did pain medication dosages and subsequent side effects. The intensity upped its volume at every turn.

All this, the beginning of that new path God had shown me. He was preparing me. The new route was a forewarning. Definitely, a rougher way.

To ease up on the commuting requirements to and from our hospital, we arranged some basic assistance with home care. We'd been taught to flush Sadie's PICC line and were careful to follow our well-taken notes. Employing caution, we avoided touching or breathing on that one stubborn postsurgical wound that refused to heal, and we kept our conversations above the weight of heavy hearts. Usually with something of humor, some fun gossip, or even some wisecracking jokes. Like, what enhancements could be made in chemo wards to make things more comfortable?

Sadie had many ideas. With toes stretched apart and wiggling to admire a recent pedicure, she offered up, "I think they should provide all the patients with oversized fuzzy slippers."

"And robes," I added.

"Yes, big comfy ones, all complimentary, of course." Her finger waved in agreement. Then her eyes brightened. "In every shade of pink imaginable!" Then her posture reclaimed a serious stance. "But of course, to avoid disappointment, patients must order their size and shade in advance. That's only fair."

I grinned. "Always thinking how to make things easy for everybody, honey. I like that about you."

She leaned back in her recliner, finger waving in sync with the inevitable swirls in her head. "Private rooms with electric buttons to darken the lights and pumped-in audio with music genres—songs that linger happily in your head."

"Or relax to help sleep," I suggested. "But you're on a roll."

"Hey, even audiobooks! Ones that remember where you left off, so when you come back a week later, it starts up at just the right spot." She pumped herself upright. "Oh, and how about movies like in first class on a plane!"

"When have you had the luxury of flying first class? And stay still," I whispered. We had yet to carry out the final step of clamping and taping up the long-term IV line "like a pogo stick."

"I got a good one. You'll like this one, Mama." She smirked. "Tuxedoed men offering poolside drinks! Of course, they'd be made with healthy stuff, like ones with protein and spinach, but miraculously, they'd be delicious."

She was right. I couldn't stop laughing. "Yeah, that's a good one for the comment box." We applauded each other with high fives.

After deep sighs that followed bouts of hearty chuckles, Sadie admired a scene formation outside our living room picture window. A cloud band stretched wide and thin. Its impression was much like a floor to an expansive upper room that filled the sky. "I hope they are having a meeting up there, discussing and deciding that I'll be allowed to stay a long time here on earth."

*Me too.* Why was God taking us on this arduous path? The detour resembled a mocking, an abandoned haunting. We were doing our best to make light of every weary footstep, despite all the pits and rocks. But that skyscraper window ledge had pushed my nervous system into a permanent on-guard state.

I adjusted my prayers, taking more care and caution in the content, always adding in the request that it would be God's will to heal Sadie. The Stop message lingered disturbingly. He obviously wasn't a big fan of whining.

When I awoke to a vision days later, my heart lightened a much-needed level—

The backdrop, so full of bright light. It shot a warm mirth straight into the marrow of my bones. A gentle wind stirred blurs of green and blue, a field of plants. A telescopic lens zeroed in on one of the flowering bushes, its focus on a single miniature blue rose and its equally tiny circular leaves. Perfect were the curves of each petal, velvet and delicate. The stunning blue was deeper than any ocean, further reaching than the clearest sky.

A knowing came. The purpose of the vision was less to signify the beauty of nature, rather the significance of the striking pigmentation.

After that, I took the stairs down two at a time to our computer on the main floor. Blue roses? No such thing, right?

Unless science played with nature, blue was not a natural color for a rose, yet that field was chock-full of them! Smiling at the thought that it could be one of the zillion beautiful sites in heaven, I took to Google. Though the internet had proven its content was not always trustworthy, surely, a blue rose was a common symbol for something.

As I suspected, since blue roses didn't naturally exist, their meaning represented a number of things, depending on the website. Mystery and attaining the impossible for one. Hope for a miracle or something miraculous to happen for another. And the third, I liked as well, was the significant tie of blue roses to the heavens, to intuition, and to the ethereal. All three, particularly the latter, provided the confidence that God was still close. He hadn't abandoned us on this tricky path, and we had plenty of reason for the hope of an *absolute* miracle.

Hah! Sadie would be healed!

# 14

Sadie, admitted to the local hospital once again, thanks to the ugly side effects of yet another new chemotherapy drug. A fresh scan completed, followed by a double whammy of news. The regimen hadn't just enabled tumor growth, but a new one had taken root. Bone growing bone.

"It's one of the most painful forms of tumors," the emergency room doctor said.

*Like we didn't know that.*

I mentally apologized for the sarcasm, even though it was just a quiet thought.

It was the era of the great oxy push. Every corner we turned, another prescription was insisted on, just different dosages.

A flash vision intruded as I sat in a waiting room. Numbers and letters signifying a Scripture verse.

2 Samuel 22.

Having zero clue what that verse was about or countless others for that matter, I shook my foot about anxiously, waiting for the opportune time to look it up when Wi-Fi was accessible. In the meantime, I hung onto that sea of bushes with the plethora of small blue roses.

*Thank you, God, for that spectacular hint.*

Sadie was admitted for severe neutropenia. The risk of infection was high. She wanted me to stay the night, so of course, I did, with permission from the head nurse and with a promise to mask the entire time. By now, I was quite used to sleeping in uncomfortable surroundings—I'd slept for hours in those straight-backed wooden staking chairs. All of it, pure luxury, the notion of complaining the furthest from my mind. My daughter lay in a bed two feet away—lungs needing air, veins craving healthy blood, neck aching from the muscle pulled by the aggressive tumor on her shoulder blade, a network of nerves desperate for a sense of calm.

An annoyed look flared in her eyes. My dear girl would rather be home.

*Me too.* "I'm sorry, honey. We have to stay here tonight."

Was it resignation or some form of resilience? How was it that Sadie wasn't startled by the failures her body had to deal with, only the inconveniences? I hoped my own eyes didn't reveal the fear stirring about in my stomach.

Comfort could only come once my daughter found sleep and reprieve, thanks to the pain meds. Then, like a warm blanket, I wrapped myself inside divine thoughts, those that assured me that, somehow, someday, all would be well.

But what's with 2 Samuel 22? It was rather odd. "David sang to the Lord the words of this song when the Lord delivered him from the hand of all his enemies and from the hand of Saul."

A lengthy verse followed, describing an Old Testament battle and subsequent praise for the win.

How on earth did God relate that to our situation? Were invisible enemies circling, like some kind of hunting game? Or rather, were they residing within—like a cancer—the kind carrying out insidious havoc with Sadie's bones and lungs and God only knows where else.

While I couldn't relate to the intensities of all the narratives, it brought to mind my own enemy. Hadn't that decades-ago Clair woman seen evil eyes watching me? God set King David back on a straight path. Was he telling me I was "bent"? Perhaps God would rid us of our enemies—that dang cancerous growth—and smoothen out our road.

At least I could cherish the final words in the verse of 2 Samuel 22: "He (God) shows unfailing kindness to his anointed, to David and his Descendants forever." Technically, as biblical genealogy reveals, that included us.

I ground my teeth beneath my mask. Here's the rub—I didn't feel so blessed right then. We had a long way to go yet to make it to that safe spot in Egypt. Such hospital stays stalled our journey.

A symbolic Egypt, I hoped that meant a place of refuge. I wasn't sure. Mary took Jesus there when he was a baby to protect him, then brought him back when danger had passed. So, I'd have to go with that. We, too, shall return to our lives when this cancerous risk had been mitigated.

My eyes admired Sadie sleeping with such peaceful soundness, albeit drug-induced. As the sweetness of her face captivated me, an anger surged with accusation. Why did I waste so much time in this private "upper room" I'd created within myself? The flooding visions and dreams filling my head were so overwhelming. Either they'd sink me or… might they be keeping me afloat? Was it my unraveling, a drowning in my sense of existence, or were they some kind of divine safety net? Should I hold them as truth? That meant I'd have to believe—and accept—there were indeed enemies. Invisible ones. Ones who wanted to harm.

The reality just two steps away in that hospital bed was daunting. I wanted to scream, to cry, to expel my internal organs. Did God not understand how hard this was? The physical weight of my head could collapse into my hands, but where shall the weight of my heart fall?

I settled on the fact that David in the Bible was eventually freed. God had intervened with perfect timing.

*So then, God, you must come just in time to save my Sadie too. Why else show me that Bible verse reference, displaying such capable power?*

Saul's behavior in that Scripture verse plagued me, though. Disobeying God made him an enemy and caused him to be despised by God. God asked me to stop praying for what I was pleading for, Sadie's healing. So was I Sadie's Saul? Surely, God wasn't suggesting that. I prayed I'd come to understand this connection.

The nurse checked in. Careful not to awaken Sadie, she took vitals and offered up smiling eyes beneath her mask. She probably noticed a soggy redness above mine, since she handed me a new one.

I nodded my thanks. The interruption was another reality check. Beeps and bed creaks, rhythmic blood pressure monitors, the shuffle of soles in the hallway, all arousing.

The battle was right here in front of me, and it was *not* invisible. *This* was real.

I called a spade a spade. I was overthinking. Overreacting. Coming undone. A parent believed they should keep their children safe. I couldn't. I hadn't. Perhaps the psyche of my mind was fired up with all these notions.

So I waved it all away.

Except, wait. What about Jake? That unsettling, haunting visitor.

*Dang.*

He'd been real.

And so had all those invisible ax-head terrors decades ago.

# 15

Hours, days, and weeks carried on without much change in direction. Small battles occasionally won and followed with celebration. The war, however, wasn't painting a win anywhere near the horizon. The roots of faith and trust burrowed deeper and deeper, thus producing foliage above ground to provide some relief from the uncomfortable, burning fears. God had us in his hands, and I wasn't about to allow myself a fall.

Though I did notice my breathing had changed. Measured and frequent, deep inhales, slow exhales. Meditation was my refuge and defense against panic, a way to stay anchored.

*This will all pass. God will never just take my child. Keep hope. Stay still. Wait it out. He has a purpose. A plan.*

A brief discussion with an oncology nurse planted an idea after I pushed on about the topic of miracles to various healthcare staff, including the janitor, whom we had gotten to know well. Had they ever witnessed one?

"Oh yes. There was one time." Nurse Lanna gave a slow nod. "You might get the charge nurse at the clinic to tell you about it. She was there that day."

Come shift change, I cornered her in the hallway to the infusion clinic. She braced against the wall, one hand on her hip as she looked me over. "Do I have your word you won't tell the others I told you this?"

My nod came quick, my breath holding in my lungs. "Yes, yes, yes, please tell me."

"One time… I swear by it—the complete disappearance of the disease. It was unexplainable, medically and scientifically, anyways. Uncanny."

I shivered, my hair standing on end at the way she said that word—*uncanny*, her head jerking back and forth, her gaze faraway as if she were recalling the situation firsthand.

"Again, remember you won't say I was your source?"

Another nod. A quick intake of breath. Then I waited.

"The patient, a middle-aged man, lungs full of lesions, his brain giving way to a resident tumor, was destined for his final day of breathing in less than a few weeks." Her arms crept around her middle. "He arrived for his check-in unusually spry and spirited and announced his eagerness for the scan results because he was sure he'd been healed."

Healed. How I longed for that.

She tsked. "Well, I must admit, a pitiful amusement filled the small examination room." The woman let her arms slide, limp, at her sides. "He reported he'd gone to some 'healing room' where a countless number of people prayed over him. He had claimed it not only felt like the weight of a rock was lifted from his head, but that a shadow, black and formless, exited his body. 'Shot out like an arrow,' he said."

I sucked in a quick breath, one hand pressed to my chest.

Her eyes glazed. Then with a steady gaze and a headshake, she shrugged. "His tests proved clear. The man's tumor—gone. No indication of the disease. His blood and scans—all normal. Never saw him again."

"Thank you for telling me." I patted her arm. "I promise I won't say you did."

I took to Google right away. Did my city have any so-called healing rooms?

I found one.

With a single thumbs-up from Sadie and two open minds, off we went. I hesitated at first. Taking Sadie out into the evening's cold air was not a good idea, but this was imperative. This avenue had to be explored. The local healing room was holding a late-night meeting across town, and of course, the sky was midnight black with an eerie, icy rain. Go figure.

Acknowledging the unfamiliarity of what to expect, we agreed we'd do anything to get a healing. A new hope surged.

I clutched Sadie's hand after I parked on the main street, a city block down from the address given, the closest we could get. Well, the closest spot with street lighting, that is. I didn't want to park in the nearby darkened lot. The rain had stopped. Still, the sidewalk glared back at us with an ominous sleekness. When we reached the five-story commercial building, its glass and metal doors were locked.

"Great. Now what?" Sadie asked.

A handwritten paper sign taped inside the window suggested the side door. "I guess we head down there?"

So down the sandwiched alley alongside the building we went. We went further than I was comfortable with, and an uneasiness prompted an inkling to turn around. At best, I could see no one lurking in the dark, a needling reminder of my basement-apartment days years ago. We were, after all, in what some eagerly described as the sketchy end of town. A protruding metal bar stuck out from the brick just ahead.

"Good. The side door's right there." I squeezed Sadie's hand, a pretense to help support her.

We scooped ourselves inside before any shadow could catch

up, and the well-lit interior hinted we were on track. Still, no healers were in sight, though another scrap of paper, this one taped to the wall, penned an arrow showing the way. The heat blasted with vigor into the hallway.

Sadie undid her coat buttons. "At least we won't be sitting in the cold."

Around the corner, yet another taped paper message affirmed our course, Healing Room Open 8:00–10:00 p.m.

She snickered. "I hope the results aren't temporary like their offices seem."

One more corner turn. Then I stopped. "Well, there it be, an open door."

And a waiting room with at least half a dozen people.

Sadie looped her arm through mine, hugging it close and leaning on me more than usual. "Success for our secret little mission!" she whisper-cheered.

But was it? "Yes, we got here." I hoped for more success than that, though. "Now, we just have to wait."

That man, supernaturally healed of his brain tumor, was our momentary trailblazer.

Everyone in the room kept to themselves. There was no chitchat, no coffee table with an array of magazines, no green plastic plants in the corners. All heads down, hands on laps. No one looked up as we entered and approached two seats together across the cramped room. Perfect. We sat like strangers invading a weighty silence. I fought the physiological urge to clear my throat while I untangled a few thoughts.

Sadie leaned on me. "What happens next? I mean, what would I say should a receptionist appear? 'Oh, hello, we're here to be miracle-ized.'"

That was my Sadie, still had her sense of humor intact. I slid my arm around her waist. "Hah, sounds absurd."

But my baby had a point.

*God, please, be with us, protect us. I pray I'm doing the right thing.*

Then it became obvious why everyone was rooted in stillness. All were aware of the considerable groaning and mumbling beyond a hollow wood door. Not to mention the odd howl, which cost me a few deep swallows. I'd heard about Christians mysteriously speaking in tongues. Even so—what was happening in that room?

Sadie elbowed me. "Mom?"

Her face said it all. What on earth?

I shrugged. I couldn't answer. I didn't know.

Then, of course, she started with the giggles.

I elbowed her back and whispered in her ear. "This is serious. They've gotta be on to something. I think they know God better than we do. Don't laugh."

But when those dimples dented her cheeks and her eyes glowed with a sparkling mischief, I struggled to stifle my amusement.

Shame on me. I felt awful after that. If I'd come to believe a battle was truly going on—one that only God could win—then I had to face this realism that some people were much further beyond in their understanding than I'd ever imagined. And they just might be the ones who could move along our healing.

Healing. Desperation took another rampant race in my bloodstream.

After get-it-together nods to each other, we stilled the jiggles in our chests, waited, and avoided each other's eyes to keep from bursting into another nervous bout, all while listening to the strange sounds coming from the next room. The room they were preparing for our miracle.

Another hurting individual arrived. He went straight to a pile of papers atop a square table. "Shoot," I whispered. "How'd I miss that?"

He completed a form and placed it in a basket, and I jumped up to be next in line. We needed to do that too.

The form requested details, a description of what type of healing we sought. My pen shook as I scribbled the weighty words—*to rid my child of cancer.*

I left the form upside down along with the others in the stack, then sank back into my chair, my heart thumping. Could it be this simple, just fill out a form?

Wait. Oops. I returned to the table, picked up our completed form, and added the words *for good.* To rid my child of cancer for good.

I'd take a temporary miracle, but I much preferred a permanent one.

A short, middle-aged woman wearing jeans and a T-shirt and sporting a cropped hair bob entered from the hallway, scooped up the completed forms, then disappeared just as quickly.

If this worked, every cell of my being would be forever grateful.

"Ah, come on, Mama." Sadie slumped. Anxiety was nabbing at her patience. "Let's just go."

"No. Not yet." I squeezed her hand gently. How I cherished having her hand in mine. "Let's give it a chance." Something niggling deep inside was excited about the possibilities.

Finally, after we'd been advised by that same woman that a few would go in before us, our turn came. Thank heavens, because my daughter had made her suggestion more than a couple of times.

The hollow wood door opened, and a different woman, this one taller with more stockiness, motioned to Sadie. We both stood, my pull of eagerness wrapped in unease.

"No." The woman raised her palm. "Just her."

My head shook without any consultation with my brain. No, they couldn't take my daughter into that room, not when I had no clue what happened in a healing room.

"No! Mama, you're coming with me, or I'm not going." Sadie was adamant.

So, *now* all the people in the waiting room lift their nosy heads?

The woman's gaze transferred from my daughter's face to mine and back again, obviously considering our strained and alert facial expressions. Twisting her mouth about, she stole a sigh. "We don't usually take two at a time."

"I'll stand back. I'll just watch," I promised.

Her apprehensive look placed me on guard. Did she think I was a nonbeliever, that I'd harm the process? I assured myself of my faith. I talked to God all the time, so I shouldn't feel doubted like that. Still, an internal battle roared. Why did this woman look at me like I wasn't trustworthy? My daughter was now eighteen. Okay, yes, an adult by many rights. Still, she was *my* child. My baby, whose life was being threatened for no apparent reason. It was my duty to find ways to protect her, so if this was an avenue to explore, we would pursue it. And I intended to ensure we kept moving forward. Together.

Hand in hand, we followed her into that room, which was now quiet. Cleansed, I supposed. Was there a darkness inside me or inside Sadie? Were we contaminating their space?

*Get a grip, Hanna! Stop such spiral thinking.*

A single stackable chair held position midroom. Seven people lingered around it. The bob-cut woman motioned to my daughter to sit. Catching a look from the tall one, I stood back and waited for some kind of instruction. Then, with no indication of a change in attitude, smiles came from both women, and I was invited into the group now forming around my seated child, who was anxiously circling her thumbs on her lap, fingers interlaced with a tense pressure. *Huh, just like Gramma Liesel used to.*

"What is your name, child?"

"Sadie," she squeaked.

"Have you both been baptized?" the tall one directed the gentle inquiry my way.

"Yes, of course," I replied. "As an infant, I was baptized, and then I underwent the confirmation-of-baptism process as a teen." It had been a matter of family tradition. I beamed Sadie's way. "She went through the same confirmation process just a few years ago."

Sadie fingered the ring with the tiny diamond on her right hand, the one I gave her after her confirmation ceremony. Then she tossed a smile my way. Good, she was starting to relax.

And so should I.

The bob-cut woman touched my forearm. It felt genuine and safe. Safe in the spiritual sense, to be precise. My exhale reminded me how anxious I was, an emotion she likely read from the tight muscles in my neck. Of course, my clenched jaw and closed fists might have said so too.

"Here's what happens next," she explained. "We will surround your daughter with praise and prayer requests."

Wasting no time, they circled and began singing. They sang,

and they smiled. They raised their hands high, each moving in a mode the Spirit granted. As the third hymn ended, they invited me in closer. We all placed our hands upon Sadie's head.

*Here it comes.* The request we'd been waiting for. And plenty of tears.

*God, I pray you are paying attention. Please watch. Please listen. Please, please take action.*

Each one of the seven prayed fervently, all at the same time. Some loud, others quiet. One broke out into a gentle hum.

I watched, not wanting to disrupt any good vibes.

My daughter's eyes searched for mine.

I nodded in return what I hoped was a sense of assurance, albeit a soaking-wet one. It felt safe. An experience I wasn't familiar with, but at the same time, one I anxiously counted on. Something miraculous needed to happen. I was hopeful. I chose to believe.

"May we recite the baptism prayer?" the bob-cut woman asked.

I found myself a little on the defensive. Hadn't I already said she was baptized? *Relax.* "Could you tell me what messages are in your prayer?"

I must've sounded like a skeptical soul. The whole experience was unlike anything I'd experienced in my traditional church upbringing, so I needed to know more. The rest of the group was patient, happy to continue praying over my daughter while the woman took me aside to recite the words.

There was nothing contrary to what I believed, or what I would have heard in our church, though I caught one slight difference—that the Holy Spirit come *within oneself* versus the *upon oneself* that I had been familiar with. A technicality?

*But what if that technicality was serious? Might God be that picky?*

*Relax,* this time my inner voice spoke louder than its last coaxing scold.

My daughter, trusting me, continued to sit, eyes closed, though seemingly taking it all in. Yes, she'd turned serious and was counting on a miracle too.

Then the baptism recital began. My daughter responded with her acceptance to believe. Nothing like an explosion occurred. Not sure what I expected. Then more hymns circulated, their notes filling all air pockets in the room.

In the middle of one hymn, my daughter cried out, "Enough! I want to go now."

She was visibly anxious, her legs shaking. The group stepped away, though one gentleman took me aside. "Might it be she is suffering because of what someone else did. Perhaps from long before her time?"

I shivered. "Could that even be possible? An invisible enemy wanting to settle some kind of score from days gone by?" I refused to absorb such a consideration. My only concern was Sadie. Sadie wanted to go, so we'd end this and leave.

"Sickness can simply result from living in a fallen world, sometimes personal sin, or sometimes be permitted by God for His purposes," he added. All given thoughts for later.

One woman helped my daughter up from her chair. Tears were flowing, not just from Sadie but also from many of those praying. I responded with meek thanks. At least I think I did. Sadie said nothing. We left the room, deposited a few twenties into the jar on that small table, and navigated our way back to the car, where we sat beneath the streetlamp.

"Well?" I asked. "Anything?"

She lowered her head into her hands.

"Oh my. I'm so sorry, honey. It's something we needed to try."

"They kept asking Jesus to forgive my sins. Mama, I don't do bad things. Why do they think I do?" She seemed angry, yet she cried even harder.

We hugged. I convinced her she wasn't a bad person, that was not why she got cancer, which was the message she took to heart. Incorrectly, I might add. It didn't seem the time to muddle through the mysterious connection between sin and sickness, especially since I'd just accepted that was simply church talk.

The experience had upset her.

"We don't have to go back." I palmed the tears from her cheeks.

She shook her head. "I want to go back. I felt something. My legs, they were, like, on fire. The heat was coming up my body. I *want* to go back, maybe in two weeks."

I didn't know where the "two weeks" came from, but that was okay. We headed home and settled in for another long night of physical suffering and painkiller infusions. We prayed together, as that was our regular habit since her diagnosis.

Sometimes, all I could do was watch and admire the way she prayed so earnestly. Speaking to God as though he were such a dear, good friend. An authoritative one she looked up to, one who held all the cards. I would melt if she pleaded with me like that. How could he turn down her requests?

Acts 14:22 says, "We must go through many hardships to enter the kingdom of God."

It's part of the journey. Hardships and battles, trials and tribulations. Whatever. I wasn't sure how to label all the disruptive and challenging boulders we encountered on our path. All I knew was that we needed God to get around them all.

It was between him and me to lift them and toss them aside so Sadie could get through this unforgiving mountainous pathway.

# 16

Two weeks went by. The trek for us was unending. Would we ever get to our destination, our place and time for God's miracle? Where the disease would be no more, where Sadie could be free of affliction and protected from enemies. Home care aids began to poke holes in my mindset, challenging my optimistic perspective.

I had to defend myself countless times today. They wanted to stuff us into their simple process chart—How to Die Well, of all things. Their questions proved they were assessing which box to place us in. Well, guess what? We weren't going in a box!

Didn't they realize I was aware of the dangers of denial? But there's a big difference between that and sustaining hope—the true kind of hope, the kind your belief system jumps into wholeheartedly. And for heaven's sake, I knew full well what the medical stakes were. I spent hours investigating clinical trials south of the border. Including stem cell transplants, which appeared to be worth considering. I'd even had discussions with our oncologist about such opportunities.

Still, I found myself defending my position to many onlookers. They confused my confidence in God with the rejection of reality. The frustration was something I'd had to shove away. The views of such bystanders couldn't make a dent in my priority list. I wasn't avoiding the seriousness of my daughter's condition by any means. Instead, though, I knew one of God's gifts to the wanting mankind was hope. And I took that gift and hung onto it tight. It was my right to do so, as I often repeated.

When I refreshed Sadie's designer water bottle and brought it to her with her favorite fish crackers to take alongside a dose of medications, she had a quiet intensity in her eyes. Still and narrow. Something deliberate was swirling inside that head of hers. "Mama, I want to see the healing-room ladies again."

"Oh?" Surprised, I crouched beside her.

"Yes." She nodded her affirmation while popping a cracker into her mouth.

She looked so comfy in the electric overstuffed recliner that had become her throne in our living room for some time now. Picking the tail end of a cheddar fish off her buttoned-down fleece pajamas, she poked away at the red-heart designs since the crumb jumped at each attempt. During one sleepless night, we'd counted them—the pajamas, that is. She had over a dozen pairs. She had debated whether to categorize them in order of color preference or degree of cuteness. The latter won.

I dared not say it. But in her weakened condition, getting her to another meeting across town in the evening's wintry air wasn't wise, nor was sitting in a small and crowded waiting room with snuffling noses. The vulnerability of her white blood count needn't have any more risk layered upon it.

Curious I was, so I implied a conclusion. "Then there was something to it? You really felt something."

"I liked them. They were nice."

"Needs to be more than that."

"I can't explain why." She scrunched her face, obviously trying to pin it down herself. "But I really want to see them again."

Pleased, I patted her fleecy shoulder. "I felt it myself. The men and women in that healing group had an admirable faith, one that couldn't be shaken."

"Like concrete." She brushed the last crumb from her pajamas. "Wait, no. Concrete cracks. More like a slab of iron."

And I had to admit I was finding myself weakening in spirit as of late. My soul required some serious refreshment. I pushed to my feet. "Let's see if they'll come to us. I'll go find their number."

Sadie beamed as I wondered if that were a natural thing—healing rooms making house calls.

I hunted up the phone book and called the number, Sadie's ears on high alert. Her shoulders sloped as I hung up after leaving a message. "They'll call back," I assured her. "Sounded like the woman with the short bob-cut, and I suspect it was her home number since it gave options to leave messages for their kids."

"What is it?" I had to ask since Sadie's quizzical mouth was twisting about.

"She has kids. I wonder if they're my age. I wonder if that makes it hard for her to see me."

My heart sank. My precious girl was worried about the woman's feelings.

Sure enough, a return call came only moments later.

After I explained our situation, I held still as I asked, "Would your group ever consider a house call?"

"Oh my." Her in-drawn breath whuffed in the receiver. "Normally, ah, we don't. 'Course, no one has ever asked for that before."

I waited, praying.

Then came her soft laugh. "You know what? I'm pretty sure I can get a few together who'd be happy to come to your home."

A knot loosened inside my chest. "Thank you. This will make Sadie so happy, and of course, me too."

As arranged, three women arrived the next morning and circled Sadie in her recliner, singing hymns, praising Christ, and pausing to call out clips and phrases as the Spirit led them.

My heart warmed over seeing Sadie so relaxed. Anxiety and doubt were absent. She was enjoying this. That, in itself, was so gratifying.

I joined in and soon felt the beatific joy Sadie must've been absorbing. A good fifteen minutes later the hymns and praises were still going strong. As sure as the sky was blue, a flutter of white left my daughter's body, the rush of air caused us all to step back, given its force. So amazing, so real. Something spiritual and supernatural was happening.

Sadie burst out in a horrific cry, another bout of pain attacking.

We all stopped to calm her. "A breakthrough dose?" I awaited her nod. Once she gave it, I'd run off for that pill as I did whenever a pain flare-up occurred.

Instead of nodding, she kept shaking her head. "No, no."

Then what?

Her weight shifted forward in her recliner, her feet banged with a restlessness, and her good arm reached out.

Panicked, I grabbed it and clasped that hand to slow her rapid wave. "We'll stop, honey. We'll stop."

How could I have arranged all this, thinking it would be good for her? What was wrong with my abilities as a proper caregiver? What kind of mother was I?

Sadie shook her head wildly and released the cause of her

collapsing physique. "I'm not crying because of pain. I'm crying because... *I feel... so... good!*"

I gasped. My mouth must've formed something, but my tongue refused to let out anything remotely vocal. I kneeled in front of her and caught her gaze. "Really?"

She nodded and, in a heartbeat, sobbed.

The women left, knowing the emotional energy bank had been fully spent. In fact, I'd say overdrawn.

Might that flutter of white we all witnessed—an angel, for certain—make his way straight to God, to report and intercede? Once Sadie settled, the debrief confirmed it—those few seconds felt like a dawning bliss. Her eyes glowed as she attempted to describe how she'd never felt so free and so good, *ever*. "I wish I could be like that all the time, and not this!" She strummed her body.

All anxiety, fatigue, and pain were back in place in her body, the home they came to play in and rest at their pleasure.

We had a quiet afternoon, both reeling in our thoughts.

Sadie had a taste of God's goodness. That's what I think. The question was this: *God, how can we get to you all the time, forever put this pain and horror behind us, and just be left with the wonderful essence of you?*

## 17

My prayer life increased. It had nearly become an hourly event. I worked harder at thoughtful, practical, and intelligent requests and employed caution to avoid the temptation of begging and pleading.

The Stop image never strayed far from my mind. My focus stayed on current requirements, things to get us through the day, sometimes merely through the next moments, so we could stay safely on course. That narrow and treacherous path was winding its way alongside unmerciful cliffs.

But I couldn't shake a feeling that something was wrong—aside, of course, from Sadie's ill-health. Through the faith of those women, God had come close. He gave Sadie a warm hug, then just up and left. It wasn't even gentle, that abrupt leaving. We were so close to something big, yet something serious was missing in my relationship with him, something held us back from whatever could make our path easier.

If I could get absolutely right with God, all this cancer business would dissolve into thin air. Poof! It would have to. Wouldn't it? Wasn't that the stuff he promised? Wasn't that what he was trying to show us?

This morning, I just poured it out.

*Hey, God, forgive me for everything I've ever said, done, and thought that I shouldn't have. And too, for everything I haven't said, haven't done, or haven't thought that I should have.* I tried to cover all the bases. *I am no saint, and I've done some pretty dumb and selfish, immature things in my time. But, honestly, I'm not a bad person.*

I even asked him if there were rules I crossed. Was it my way of life, my poor decisions or poor behaviors, my failed relationships? I missed the boat, took a wrong turn somewhere.

My weedy root of accusation was healthy, given its decades of growth. And just why was that my automatic go-to? Familiarity? If somebody else was wrong, I must be right? A false sense of control?

I insisted on blaming the quiet ruin from the wreckage during childhood. This life I built upon scars was not my ideal. Certainly not the model of a perfect Christian woman. "It's not my fault!" I waved a fist at the ceiling. Still, the inkling that God might be judging me struck a chord. As if that could be the reason for this punishment. But fear of God was greater, and a heartfelt apology came almost immediately.

Days later, a startling awakening struck.

A deluge of emails had piled up. I couldn't avoid them forever. Interrupting a lengthy update to a friend came a disturbing vision. My skin prickled, and I jerked back, then sat upright. At attention and guarded. What terrible thing had I done now? An image consumed the wall behind the computer screen. My fingers lifted from the keyboard just as it—and the monitor—were swallowed into nothingness. There it be, him. A shoulder clothed in white. A forearm, his left. An ominous presence.

I don't recall breathing.

"God?" I'm not sure if my lips moved when I dared the ask.

The arm flung outward with harsh boldness. *Away with you!*

An action impossible to challenge.

An image of myself then hurled through a space of foggy gray. So small and inconsequential was I.

Pure terror chilled me. "No! Why are you tossing me away?"

God's left side was reserved for his enemies. Like a scrap of garbage, my body floated down, discarded.

Regret, panic, fear, all indescribable. The horror of an overwhelming dread. Was this irreversible?

This simply couldn't be.

My hands wrapped tight around my neck, a meager attempt to soothe the goose bumps.

Dare I run or continue to watch?

My image fell to a hard, barren ground. The implication of a harsh hit. My own body jolted.

This topped it. Never had I been so spiritually disoriented. So very frightened. This was not the God I knew.

*Best not move. Just breathe.*

A new scene unfolded. And changed my life.

I recognized it in an instant. Feet, bare and bronze. I saw now where God tossed me. I lay as a criminal, a broken being, at the feet of Jesus pinned to his cross.

Jesus. His child.

The one he watched suffer.

*And now I am.*

His feet pulsed, and a fresh droplet of blood oozed onto the ground.

I had never felt so humiliated. Casting a look up to glance at the face of Christ was not an option I dared to consider. It was painfully obvious.

I did not *know* him, that divine and cherished Son of his. A stranger.

# 18

*Your ego is obvious.*

The phrase from so many months ago looped like a merry-go-round. Only more like a horror-go-round.

I called myself a Christian, even believed it. Pride—one of the things God hates the most. And I had been full of it. I sidestepped Christ all through my life.

Other than repetitive phrases in church, I had never prayed to Jesus per se. It was always God. I always thought it best to, well, go straight to the top. When discussing religion with friends, I found it easy to argue, citing assurances that there were many ways to God. Even though I claimed it was my upbringing and thus my preferred route, I insisted Christ was just one road to heaven. It was my way of acknowledging and respecting all religions, leaving Jesus on the side, as though he were simply roadkill.

*Bad decision.* How could I have been so off track, so foolish with my reasoning?

Even one of the healing-room women had corrected me in a conversation. I referred to the name of God to pursue the healing.

But she'd shaken her head. "Jesus," she had said.

I chuckled deep inside at the time, thinking, "Maybe *you* go to Jesus; *I* go straight to God."

This was a lesson I would never release. Believing in God

without believing and accepting his Son was indeed the truest definition of pride. If he hadn't shown me that dramatic toss-away show, would I have figured it out for myself?

That new foundation I'd been working on just blew up.

It is said, "The fear of the Lord is the beginning of wisdom" (Proverbs 9:10).

God injected some of that alarm into my bones. Yet also, a new beginning in my heart. It took a few calls using the name of Jesus before the embarrassment and shame disappeared. I had known *of* him, even taught about him in Sunday school, read about him, and sung his name. None of that mattered. I needed to *know* him. To "know" in a biblical sense referenced a close relationship, commitment, and loyalty.

I focused on this significant missing connection, but where to start?

I swallowed what God had shown me: a firm truth, my need for Christ. *Believe it.*

The Gospel of John became my favorite book in the Bible. Being rich with spiritual intimacy, its words capable of stirring and anchoring at the same time.

Within weeks, my vision life produced great rewards, and a beautiful and powerful scene unfolded —

This one was different. I was one of the characters. Well, I never saw my face, but I knew it was me.

Dressed in flowy white attire, I was part of an exciting wedding celebration. A canopy stretched across the festivities. Above that, an endless sea of stars. I wasn't the bride, but a bridesmaid.

Jesus grabbed both my hands and swung me around. We danced and danced.

Then he walked me toward the bride's table. First, we'd have to pass in front of a master table, starting on the tent's south side, moving to the north end.

I hesitated. Fear stopped me, my legs crippled in weakness.

A fierce four-legged beast snarled, its sharp, bloodstained teeth straining to reach me. A collar surrounded his neck, but the handle of his leash lay flat and unattended on the ground. Although not secured by any physical restraint, it didn't lunge. An unseen authority forced it to stay in place, and a guard at its sides ensured its obedience.

Jesus motioned me to come, continue to follow him straight past the beast.

The beast's eyes were pure evil, and he growled as I managed a slow step.

It seemed the decision was up to me. To continue with the celebration of joy and brave the walk past the beast by following Jesus, or to stay put, paralyzed in fear, on the side that couldn't, or wouldn't, follow Christ.

The scene dissipated.

The wedding was Sadie's. At least, I thought so. For certain, it was a spiritual wedding. The beast disrupting our lives was captured, and I was free to stroll past it, claiming freedom from its threats. If I wanted to see the bride and partake in the beautiful food display, I had to cast my fear aside. Place all faith in Jesus.

"Come," he had encouraged.

"I'll do my best!" I whispered within, relishing the new empowerment.

The beast's image haunted me, though. It had been ready and wanting to tear my flesh apart, its four legs stiff and poised to pounce. Even its short, black spikes of shiny hair appeared tension-charged, its doglike ears perked, its long-pointed snout raised for combat.

But its infernal red, unblinking eyes and the bloody fangs terrified me beyond measure. Hatred in its rawest form. And no one held onto his leash? How disturbing!

The beast obeyed some bigger rule—it could watch; it couldn't attack. Not while Jesus was present, anyway.

And what about that psychic's alarming words from all those years ago—*"Those eyes. I don't like how he's watching you"*?

Was it that beast that she saw? I would have kicked my butt out of my kitchen too if I were her and saw that.

Physically for Sadie, things didn't change. The next month got increasingly difficult. Her pain management was more complex. A pain pump affixed with stronger medications helped, though it interfered with her rest. Physical discomfort and fatigue, constipation and anxiety were all taking their toll. More unplanned hospital trips, more mouth sores, more restlessness.

Throughout each day, I committed to self-reminders, claiming that joy and peace and all goodness were ours, encouraging Sadie however I could, be it spiritually or physically, mentally or emotionally. Our beast was Sadie's cancer. "Simply keep strolling and follow tightly behind Jesus," I coaxed us. "Never let go. Never stray. Just walk past the beast. Then all will be well."

Then a new instruction came—

God showed me a mountain. We were nearing its peak. I was leading the way, pulling Sadie higher and higher, but she was getting weaker and weaker. She was discouraged with the climb, believing God had abandoned her and she'd never reach the top. It appeared she might just quit.

I was instructed to scramble around so I would be beneath

her in the trek. It was time to switch. Up to this point, I walked a footstep in front of her in an attempt to prepare her for what I could see was coming and, possibly, clear the path.

Now, I was to walk behind her. She'd need encouragement to keep going. She was only a few steps from reaching the top of that glorious peak, and she was weary, wanting to stop. My role was to keep her from tumbling down, to assist her in finishing her race by nudging her upward.

There was plenty to unpack. A tent. A wedding. A beast. A mountain peak and a treacherous climb, no less. My spiritual life and my daughter's physical existence entwined. The whole business had a strong sense of purpose to it all. Yet I continued to live two lives. One immersed in the supernatural essence of divine mysteries; the other planted on earth in horror of what appeared to be coming. The only way through this mind-bending dichotomy was to continue to believe that healing was on its way, even as Sadie's physical health deteriorated bit by bit each day.

That famous seed of "inner peace beyond understanding" had perched inside me, sure enough. Indeed, a lovely gold nugget it was. Only, it wasn't sprawling much. Its roots wouldn't break ground, not while my daughter suffered so.

When she healed, I'd let it grow.

## 19

**It was tough** to believe this was how God chose to work in my life. I was certain he was being much harder on me than anybody else I knew. Christian-claiming individuals or otherwise. As to why, who knew? Just how could he provide such sacred unveilings and soul-deep awakenings, yet force one to witness their child's suffering?

Surely, I'd find out one day.

Snippets came forth throughout the coming days when my mind was elsewhere on the practicalities of demands, on an hour-by-hour basis. I was thankful for these brief commercial interludes, if only to refresh my energy. My favorite one—

Nature was at its peak. A row of tall trees with beautiful foliage and healthy roots reaching deep into a nearby river. Crystal-clear waters sparkled and flowed, and a whispered knowing came—one of those trees was my daughter and the one aside it, myself. Many others on each side of us, who they represented was not shared. The image brought me a full smile. God had a plan; we were part of it, as were many others. He would be sure we were nourished, his way, from his river, and I supposed my nourishment came from all these visions.

Then a long-awaited happening—

Another time, as I slept on the floor at the end of Sadie's bed, two highly transparent angels appeared. Yes, allow me to repeat myself. Two highly transparent angels entered her room straight from the ceiling. I watched them both land by her side with utter grace and silence. Harmonious and as natural as could be, slightly larger than life.

Each acknowledged me with barely a nod and went about their business. One carried a new heart and the other had an armful with two packages, a new lung in each. They hovered over a sound-sleeping Sadie, and the fluttery backside of one blinded my line of sight. Perhaps on purpose.

Was I meant to see this?

By the way the back of their elbows jabbed and moved about, their arms had to be elbow-deep in Sadie's chest. They were replacing her diseased lungs and heart with the new ones! A spiritual exchange.

I remained still and watched, and for most of it, I needed to hold tight to our cat, who'd taken to hissing fits. Ears flat against her head, her uneasy defensiveness was disturbing. Her back arched as her head moved where they did. She obviously saw them too.

To handle the wrangling, I pushed her into the hallway. Still, her paws repeatedly appeared beneath the closed door with her want back into the room.

This surgical process took such a long time that I'd fallen asleep before the celestial medical workers left. As exhausted as I was, the mystical amazement of witnessing the entire thing was wasted on me.

Though, when I awoke, as far as I was concerned her healing had, without a doubt, occurred. That vision was obvious. God came through. Sadie was gifted a new body.

Sadie had slept well that night, a pure oddity in itself. When she awoke, I assured her Jesus was working at a complete healing, she need not worry or lose faith. I was far more enthusiastic than ever to encourage and inspire her that all would, in fact, be well. God had granted his gift of hope, and we would stand firm upon his good promises. Despite the disease's apparent winning position, I was 100 percent certain she would be healed.

The next few days, I couldn't put my good mood to falter, no matter the circumstances. I could barely stand it. My gaze darted, searching through the appointment book for Sadie's next round of scans.

I just knew that'd be the day. Time for our miracle news!

## 20

OVERWHELMING EVIDENCE EXISTED, and the scans proved it. Sadie's cancer would continue to rack her body, a viper squeezing life from her bones, nerves, and veins.

*All this believing—just a hollow void. Nothing but zealous foolishness.*

I resented myself, ashamed I'd shared such ridiculous anticipation. I could have floated into eternity on a platform of bitterness. Desperate to turn my back on this God of mine, I couldn't. Sadie needed help in a whole new way—she was having nightmares, terrible ones—and only he could do something about it. Yet I begrudged asking him for help.

Horror-stricken, I listened as Sadie's shoulders quaked while her hands took turns wringing and squeezing, pulling at fingers. Right, then left, then the right again. Eyes glassy, this terrified look was a first. Because up until that moment, even in that diseased body, her eyes radiated and could splash sunshine into any room she entered. In fact, one particular home care worker, who claimed to see auras with hospice patients, shared her astonishment when she tended to Sadie. She witnessed a bright, colorful aura, explaining that in all her other patients, such was typically a dark, heavier feel.

So, seeing Sadie so disturbed was more than distressing. A nightmare so horrifying. She didn't deserve such. As she described her nightmare, I couldn't interrupt, even if I wanted to. My heart lay firm and resolute like a boulder in the middle of my throat.

"I was… lifted into the air… by someone… up through the roof and into the sky." The words came in phrases, heavy breaths in between each. "It was cool and nice… so special. Streams of… yellow light… all around. I was so free… at least at first."

I held onto her arm, grounding her.

Her head rocked side to side. "That 'someone' said nothing, and that was strange. There were no warm or comforting thoughts coming from him. It made me wonder… who was this? So… I asked, 'Is that you, Lord? Is that you?'"

My gut twisted over the hollowness in her voice, the glassiness in her frantic gaze.

"He kept pulling me… faster and faster. Oh, Mama… I was getting so nervous!"

Something must've triggered an alarm.

"I kept asking him over and over, but… the man… he wouldn't respond!" Her back arched. "Suddenly, I *knew*! It was *not* the Lord." Sadie burst into tears. "I screamed in the dream to stop. Then the man let go. I fell, free-falling, screaming all the way. Nothing to catch me! Then I… woke up."

Sheer horror shivered through me. A storm raged inside. Thankful she shared it with me, I stayed focused and continued with gentle applauding motions. "You were so smart to verify your escort. Always be sure it's Jesus. Don't be fooled."

Where my exterior calm came from, I'd no idea. This scenario was out of my league. Who was I to provide advice on the dangers lurking in the afterlife? I was no expert and wished this whole business would just blow away—all such intruding visions and dreams. I've never asked for or wanted any of it.

Another terror came soon after. Sadie described a conveyor

belt. "I couldn't see where it started. It was like a moving assembly line in a factory. I was tied to it. Couldn't move my arms or legs. The belt advanced on rollers, steady-like, and couldn't be stopped." She appeared so weary and tired. "Or at least whoever was in charge wasn't there to stop it. And the men all around the conveyor belt just stood there, laughing and rubbing their palms together. I could lift my head enough to see where I was going. Mama, I was being fed into a series of sawing blades, and they just teased me—and there was nothing I could do about it!"

She screamed at me to stop them, but I was numb. All I could do was hold her and provide consolation. It was just a nightmare.

This was no ordinary crisis. A battle between survival and the end, life versus death. Insanely unbearable. Other than comfort and assure her that she was safe now, that her mind was stirring up a nasty storm, I needed to find an answer for her. Something more truthful, not just pacifying words. The haunting threat was not something Sadie could just shake off, and I didn't want it rooting into her psyche. Most likely, these terrors stemmed from the fear of dying. And who could blame her? In some profoundly bizarre universe of psychology, such terrors were possibly normal.

God had been chasing me throughout the decades, literally pounding me over the head with a sledgehammer to get my attention—all so I'd come to know Jesus. Now that I had accepted Jesus, like a couple of kids playing tag, I was chasing him, the Son of God. Flipping through the New Testament for wisdom and explanations. Particularly now, with great need for urgency. For some mind-settling enlightenment regarding Sadie's terrors.

*I'm playing in a dangerous arena, Jesus. Seriously, I never asked for this! This has to be your battle. I'm counting on you.*

Together, we searched and contemplated a verse. 2 Corinthians 11:14 warned that even the bad guy, one we refused to verbalize his name, dressed as an angel of light. He was good at deception. Matthew 24:24 warned not to be deceived. I patted Sadie on the back, for she was not deceived.

Based on our findings, dreams could indeed come from ungodly sources, so understanding how to test them was key. Should a dream lead one astray to disobedience, rather than correction, then it wasn't from God. If it inflated one's pride, rather than bringing glory to the divine, then it wasn't from God. God-given dreams would confirm truth in the Scriptures, and though his whispers could warn, protect, correct, or guide, most importantly, his voice brought peace, not confusion (1 Corinthians 14:33).

These recent terrors of hers did *not* bring peace! That was the clincher. We could toss the terrors away. Divine permission granted—the deepest corners of our souls could obliterate any and all negative impacts.

Sadie and I prayed together, in Jesus's name. For enlightenment and for the protection of our minds and souls, to eliminate such terrifying messages of fear. The cancer was attempting to spread to all layers of existence, not just Sadie's flesh and bones.

As for this invasion attempt, that monstrous impassable obstruction in our path? Disintegrated! Sadie's eyes lit with their familiar sparkle, and her muscles softened in peaceful relief.

Several hours later, I sat in solace in my favorite place of meditation. Though amid the 3:00-a.m. darkness no streams of sun shone into the oversized windows, the hot coffee in hand comforted me as I contemplated.

*Father, you brought out the darkness in Sadie today so it could be seen. Recognized. And demolished. You gave rest to her soul. Thank you.*

# 21

**I dreamed** I brought Jesus into my home, my heart-home. The place I'd fashioned for my soul to live. As I showed him around, I examined it myself for the first time. I led him through a short hallway into an oppressive cave-like dwelling. Despite the darkness, he followed anyway, looking around, checking the place out as if it might be a place he'd care to stay. The hallway ended in a solitary window, the only eye to the outside world. A partial view lay beyond, one I sensed to be idyllic.

From where I stood, I could make out a tranquil park, half veiled by a curtain of trees. A sense of knowing completed the view with the parts I couldn't see. People gathered around picnic tables, lingering in nature, enjoying themselves. Just imagining it seemed good enough for me.

The window was cracked open a tad. And when I purposefully lent my ear, chimes danced, and laughter ballooned in the distance. As much as I wanted to catch a lovely breeze and fill my lungs with all that fresh air, I couldn't. The window wasn't in reach. Too much junk was in the way. A broken rocking chair, crates of old stuff, debris I didn't even recognize what it had once been—all of it piled along the hallway.

Why would I hang on to all this as though it were some kind of treasure? Clearing it all out would take effort, and I hadn't the energy.

So, in the dark hallway, we paused. Kinda just stared at the window from there. If only I'd cleaned up before he came!

Jesus pointed to the only other space in my heart-house, a windowless room at the side, the walls and low ceiling also rounded and cave-like. This time, he led; I followed.

The room was even darker than the hallway, given no direct light. Still, it had a cozy feel, or I thought so anyway. A couch was there, not a large one, more like a love seat. I can't recall much else, only the thick rug on a dry, packed-dirt floor. The rug offered the main attraction, an old shaggy type. Since we couldn't get to the hall window with the lovely view, we sat on the couch. Apparently, I sat there a great deal, as the dents in the worn cushions revealed.

A gnawing discouragement crept over me. Jesus was here to visit. I should be proud to show him my home and its great view. Now, it didn't feel like such a good place. Embarrassed and uncomfortable, I couldn't look at him. My hands in my lap, I swirled my thumbs around each other.

His torso shifted, and his arms reached to lift the rug, exposing the ground.

A nauseating stink clogged the room.

I flinched and covered my mouth, then my nose.

An opening right there in the floor, a festering crater. A deep, orange bubbling with a living ooze. Gross. How could a shag carpet possibly cover such a volcanic blaze, like a thick scab over an active bleeding wound? How often had I sat there, meditating even, as a hole in my heart was sealed with mere man-made fibers of polyester and nylon?

To my horror, an angry stream fired up daggers into my personal breathing space.

Jesus stooped right away. He spread both palms wide over

the chasm—and the burning orange obeyed and cooled to ashes! He maneuvered the floor of flesh, churning the dirt to a muddy mixture, and employed it to close the hole. As an expert craftsman might, he smoothed the floor to a perfect restoration, brushed off his hands, and smiled with a nod. Done.

Then a tiny flame flickered through the mud slab. The smile on his face telling. A burning reminder of this event for me to learn from. I must keep my heart-home guarded at all times. Stay in control of what I permitted to enter.

This dream cracked open a sea of memories with locked-in emotions. Recollections of guilt, flashes of anger, sensations of shame. People needing my forgiveness, people I wanted forgiveness from.

All the things I'd hidden beneath that carpet over the years had created a direct passageway of their own, inviting in whispered lies of deceit. One by one, specific emotions tied to specific moments in my life surfaced, popping like corn in a hot, sizzling pan.

This was my housecleaning. I'd shoved so much under that carpet, never mind the trash I allowed to clog the hallway, blocking the path to my one-and-only window. My feeling of inadequacy had always been a lie, only serving to do harm. Still, the weightier items wouldn't budge.

I'd get to them later.

And that carpet had to go so I could keep a better watch.

# 22

God's timing was supposed to be perfect. So why now?

Such profound insight he was giving me, identifying hidden obstacles lurking in my heart—a longing for self-validation and my regrettable tendency to feed on the fruit of a deep-rooted spirit of accusation. All significant details that were extremely helpful when one committed to switching on a self-improvement lever.

But this was not the time to be concerned with my emotional clutter. The priority was Sadie. It bugged me. Surely there wasn't a connection between the discouraging revelations of my heart and Sadie's physical illness. That would be absurd. So why was he choosing now to show me these things when I had no time or space to confront?

In the off chance of a link, I stood in my quiet bedroom and called on God. When I believed—*hoped*—he was listening, I dared my ask. "If I do my utmost to keep my heart clean from here on in, will you then heal Sadie… physically?"

With specific heavyweight items in mind, ones I could describe if not define, I wanted a deal.

No response.

Evidently, he didn't make deals.

I stood in silence. Then I sighed and criticized myself for such senselessness.

Then his voice came to my heart, "Go ahead. Ask me."

My head rose instantly.

He was listening! He knew what was really on my heart.

Okay, then. In an attempt to prepare for whatever answer he gave, I breathed in deep and held it.

Then each word emerged in a blurt. "Are—you—going—to—heal—Sadie?"

A resounding yes came.

My eyes grew big. He answered!

Why did I worry so?

An overwhelming relief invigorated every cell of my being. My lungs sank with an abrupt exhale, and my shoulders collapsed, taking my chest with them. I beamed and fell to my knees. *He said yes!*

But then a pause. He was still there. Waiting.

I'd better not waste his time.

Unfolding myself back to a stand and arching my chin upward, I counted on his presence being where I gazed.

"So, what do *I* need to do?" *Anything!*

An arm motioned for me to turn around, clockwise, specifically to my right.

"Turn around?" I obeyed, arms out wide, and turned to circle right.

*Am I to do a half circle, full circle? Take an opposite direction in life? Or simply, just look around, see for myself that I am fortunate, in a home with a roof, a closet full of clothes, and a fridge full of food. A loving family I can call my own.*

I completed a full circle just in case.

But that was it. He was gone, or so I felt. One giant step further in my spiritual life. I'd begin the cleaning-out process of my heart, but now, one frustrating step back. I'd have to contemplate this turn-around business.

No matter. He was going to heal Sadie!

# 23

Following a great sleep-in, Sadie was bursting at the seams. *She'd* had a vision.

I was eager to hear it. Such a huge relief, given those terrible nightmares a couple of weeks prior. Such fun to see Sadie so happily filled, her eyes wide with delighted wonder as she shared the details.

"Well, just like we are now, I was sitting at the eating counter right here, in our kitchen." She rested an elbow on the marble top, and her cupped hand framed the dimple from her grin. She pointed to the empty chair beside her. "And Jesus was there. He came for breakfast! No biggie." She giggled. "We were just hang'n. I went to pour my cereal, but my bowl was full of blood. 'What do I do with this?' I asked." Her palms stretched outward, and her head cocked as she demonstrated a mimic of her query to Jesus. "He didn't have to say anything—I knew what to do." She pointed her index finger straight at her chest, her smile satisfied.

My heart warmed. Just watching her animated moves as she explained her chat with Jesus refreshed my lungs with tingles of new life. The scent of love loomed inside me. "What, honey?" I placed my own elbows on the counter and leaned toward her. "What did you do?"

Sadie's eyes narrowed. "I took a sip, like at church, but this was *real* blood." She got serious and leaned in, our noses nearly touching. "Then I poured the rest over my head." She sat tall again, as far as her shoulder would allow. "I asked him to check. I wanted to be sure my whole body was covered." Her arms floated downward against each side of her body. "Didn't want to miss a spot!"

Great self-satisfaction curved her lovely, innocent face. "I gave him a paintbrush."

"A paintbrush?" I scooted back and sat tall myself.

"Yeah, well, he needed something to cover the missed spots."

"Right, of course. Good thinking!"

She turned quiet. "I hope it means I get to stay here for a long time."

"Me too," I said.

Sadie perked up. "We were both laughing." She wagged her finger as she often did to drive a point home. "I told him: 'Be double sure, no missed spots!' He likes to joke around, and he thinks I'm funny."

I hugged her and kissed her forehead. "You are funny. I think so too."

"Yeah." She giggled. "I know."

The rest of the day, all I could think of was imagining my daughter shaking her finger at Jesus with a disciplining tease—"be sure you don't miss a spot"—and the two of them laughing.

Sadie's vision was most definitely the high note of that week, and she loved sharing it with family, friends, and nurses, anyone who stopped by. Her siblings keen to coax for more details.

But why was it that she could be so courageous to verbalize her commitment to Christ, while I had such a reservedness about it? I barely spoke of my faith and never spoke about my experience with visions and dreams.

## 24

At last, the calendar flipped to March.

The goal was to get Sadie to a clinical trial that was coming to our oncology unit in just three weeks. Though right now, such timing seemed impossibly far off. She was sick and tired of being sick and tired. February's long and heavy days weighed like a cold memory one couldn't shake, and the horror of a blackness had bullied its way in. Snickering giggles and sunshiny smiles lessened. If only I could pull out that beautiful spirit of my daughter's and embrace it, hold it tight to keep it safe from the evil ravaging her body while we waited to climb the next rung in the ladder of medical hope.

Speaking of spirits, just where was Jesus? And where was that promise God made ever so clearly?

For the first time ever, I initiated a cancellation for the next day's chemo infusion, sure that Sadie's blood results would prove she wasn't up to it. Although a couple of times in the past, we had forecast a guess incorrectly. Even so, my girl was so weak, and just the thought of the hours-long drive to and from the city center was unbearable enough. Sadie pleaded not to go. But the oncology nurse insisted Sadie needed to come, and the doctor wanted to see her for himself. So, we buckled up our courage and our seat belts, and off, we went.

I pined for the good ole days when Sadie could hop out and skip up the wide set of stairs leading to the hospital's front door while I parked the car. Nowadays, we needed a driver so I could exit the vehicle with her and fetch a wheelchair.

How and when did that transition happen?

What never changed was the size of Sadie's knockoff purses. Today, she carried a white "Guess" version with silver buckles and studs. Always stuffed to the brim and plopped on her lap or within an arm's reach, a favorite stuffie with big eyes poking his head out of the top. Timon, the wisecracking something or other from *The Lion King*. Her flip phone, notepad, giant crossword puzzle book, gum and snacks, warm socks, water bottle, plus a wide assortment of other things loaded beneath Timon. She liked to be prepared.

This doctor visit was different. As Sadie lay in the bed, scrolling through her phone, I attended a meeting with the doctor. Never before had he called me over for a private meeting to chat, certainly not without his patient present. How many times had I sat through the she's-being-treated-as-an-adult-so-we-discuss-with-her-not-the-parents speech? Though that approach transitioned just like the skipping-up-the-stairs process had changed to being pushed in a wheelchair. Still, when he led me into his office, a cubby at the back of the clinic area, I knew it wasn't going to be good.

He settled into his chair and rolled it closer to me, stopping a mere foot away, holding eye contact. "Sadie isn't well enough for her chemo appointment."

"I'm not surprised." No reason to point out that I said so myself on the phone and he could've spared us this trip.

"Hanna..." He dragged my name out. "She's not well enough to qualify for the clinical trial."

What? No! Our hopes... They were pinned to that trial.

That was our next step, our last chance. I couldn't speak. If I did, it would mean I heard and digested what he said.

"I'm sorry." His voice was as steady as his headshake. "I had to remove her from the eligibility list."

The heaviness now in my chest forced me to clear my throat. I rubbed my arms but couldn't remove a sudden chill. "So then what?"

He looped his hands loosely in his lap. His shoulders dropped, perhaps from a weight lifted. This authoritative professional with exacting commands, who at first insisted we transfer to a pediatric hospital, which we refused, had been lured into the charms of young Sadie. She consistently returned his gruff and serious voice with an infectious smile and that scolding finger, announcing she was his favorite patient. Eventually, sparks of warmth danced across his facial features during their visits.

"I'm letting her go as my patient."

I gasped. My hands clenched tight to the seat of my chair. This man, our guiding medical beam of light we'd adored for eighteen months, was what? Disappearing into a sunset? Or were we the ones to disappear?

"Hanna, there's just… nothing else I can do."

I felt his gaze but could no longer look his way. I glanced at his bookshelf, at that framed photo Sadie had gifted him of him and her posing in the chemo ward hallway. She had a nurse snap it months ago. Seeing it displayed here in his office with no other photos in the room other than that of his wife stirred a smile somewhere inside me. Sadie had touched him.

"She may have six weeks."

But their good relationship couldn't save her life.

I just sat there, dumbfounded, as if he just told me it's about to rain soon. Not liking the rain, I nodded and said something mindless, like, "Okay, thank you."

I wasn't interested in whatever else he had to say. His following words blurred against the countdown. *Six weeks.* When I stood to leave, we shook hands and he added his final, quiet message. "I know you and your family will be devastated."

The walk down the hall to the room where Sadie lay might as well have been walking a plank, only with my head held high. *Better not look down.*

The news hemmed me in. If I stayed perfectly still inside this tornado, our haven, and looked only upward, all would be okay. This was just another whirling dagger. A piercing, cruel blade.

*God, did you hear all that?*

Sadie lowered her phone and gave me a look that said: "What did he say?"

Then an incoming message beeped, her gaze lowered, and her smile returned. My girl distracted thanks to social demands.

This was not a pediatric hospital, and discussions such as I'd just had happened with the patient. We fell into a crack. Pediatrics took cancer patients up to the age of seventeen, while this hospital took adults, eighteen and over. Sadie being diagnosed at seventeen created dilemmas periodically.

Early on, she made me promise I wouldn't hold back information from her. There was never to be any business where I knew something about her health she didn't know. It was her body, her life at stake.

I'd promised, and up until this moment, I'd kept that promise. She was the first to be made aware of any and all news, and communication plans were discussed many times. When discouraging news came our way, we made a pact. That's when we came up with the forty-eight-hour time limit. No more than that would we dwell or grieve. Then after, whatever the backward step delivered would be swallowed up as we moved onward. Often, we didn't require the entire forty-eight hours, though it was frustrating how many others didn't appreciate that rule. Wanting details of last month's scans or last week's test results when we'd already internalized and regrouped. Staying focused on the next singular step, no matter how minute or large, was always our priority.

Of course, everyone always meant well. We were fortunate to have so many rally around us.

This morning's meeting was different. I need to sort this confusion, let it pool and separate. I'd poke my head into the howling winds to see how sharp that dagger really was. How could I push her up that mountain if I were weighed down and blindsided by the storm?

God assured me she'd be healed, did he not?

The enemy was real. Wanting to strike and watch us bleed out. Doubt, fear, and panic swelled a taunting mixture. I sat, thankful for whatever messages were distracting my daughter.

Her phone beeped again, and her sigh slipped free, her shoulders inching up. "March break's coming. Everyone's making plans."

None would be possible for her. Frustration must be dancing upon Sadie's worn-out nerves.

She lowered the phone. "We're trying to figure out how I can still take part."

I nodded, waiting for the signal we could head home since there'd be no chemotherapy infusion—this day or ever, for that matter. I recoiled at the gravity of the God-breathed message in the back of the car before we arrived here today. Barely more than two hours ago. It had been unfittingly majestic and glorious. Not to mention, unnerving and soul-cutting—

A celebration in the heavens. Confetti streams of color everywhere, the air bursting with excited cheering. A crowd of dozens, all dressed in white with accents of various shades and hues and tints, all pushing in to get close to Sadie. A thrill of love and joy spilled from their hearts. Sadie, a young and healthy girl, basked in their midst. Excited. Smiling. Glowing with delight.

The vision was mean. Nasty. I held my hand over hers and took in her face as we neared the hospital, her skin gray, her eyes dark, her head drooped. Though not privy to seeing her aura as that home care worker claimed to, I was certain at that moment in time it was of a darkened nature.

She was sad.

I was sadder.

But in that vision—the heavens were celebrating as we sat in the back seat doing anything but. What a polar opposite. The furthest possible contrast.

This was the dichotomy of dichotomies. How could there be a divine celebration vision while my daughter was suffering so? My body stiffened and went rigid.

*No, God. My turn to say, "Stop!"*

Surely, the vision was a sign of Sadie's celebrated homecoming.

*You're taking her back. All along, you had no plans to heal her, did you?!*

Defeated, my soul allowed the hit. That hatchet swing wasn't invisible this time. It had struck with the doctor's update, a sharp and cutting blade with no mercy.

## 25

LATER THAT SAME day, the darkness of evening fell, but sleep wouldn't come. Then again, it never did. Days and nights had been switched for some time now. No matter the time the clock read, Sadie was extremely uncomfortable—be it oxygen flow, pain or anxiety management, or a host of other nasties. Simply no bodily position provided relief for any length of time. Prayers and drugs, more prayers and more drugs. Chatting and crying.

"I don't want to die, Mama," she pleaded. "Do something!"

I'd shared her disqualification from the clinical trial. I hadn't yet shared the rest of the doctor's news. That was as much as I could say. Selfishly, for a matter of hours, maybe for just tonight, I needed some meditation space. But Sadie's heart must already know—

A distraction would do us good. I plugged in a movie. We settled on *Uptown Girls*, as neither of us had seen it before. I paused the movie whenever Sadie needed to grapple with a wrenching clutch or spasm or simply change position to find some comfort. When a piercing agonized cry filled the air and there was absolutely nothing I could do, I could hold it in no longer. Not wanting Sadie to see that I'd reached my boiling point, I ran out.

Inside my laundry room, shutting the door not a second too soon, I exploded. So furious with God! What the blazes was he doing? Was this truly necessary? My fists clenched and waved with wild lunacy, slicing the air every which way possible, challenging his approach.

"God, you look at her! Right now! She prays so sweetly, so earnestly, asking you for help. And what are you doing? She's in so much pain, what the heck!" Yes, I swore at him. "She loves you. So, you get down here now, and you heal her! You've been promising this. We've been faithful to you, trusting you, never giving up hope. Get down here right now! You need to take her pain away! No more of this!"

Finally, I said my bit. He needed to hear this from me. He dared give us so many prewarnings to help us through this journey, and then he let her suffer like that? Seriously!

Once I'd drawn a few deep breaths and the heat in my veins cooled a degree, I calmly removed myself from the laundry room and returned to Sadie. Her gaze at my face appeared puzzled. She must've wondered why I had to escape.

Did she hear me punching the air with my fist? Were my howling screams not as muffled as I thought? Rage was still draining from my cheeks. Plus, the body trembles hadn't left entirely. I had, indeed, met my breaking point. How could God allow someone who loved him to go through such suffering, all while he just sat by and watched? I just didn't understand this. I couldn't accept this. Yet, no choice did I have.

At least the horrific cramping in Sadie's body subsided. I hoped there'd be a good break before the next one came—good heavens, in fact, I hoped there wouldn't be another one. At least another one she couldn't handle.

*Let me take it in her place. Please. She's weak, exhausted, and so undeserving of this.*

It took both my husband and me to get her up the stairs and

into her bed. When we neared the top step, God spoke to me. Audible words. Clear, concise, and instructive.

"It's time."

I knew what he meant.

## 26

Respecting my promise to Sadie, I had a job to do. The top priority—to have a discussion with my child. Not the one of drugs and alcohol. Not the one of self-identity and self-worth. Nor the one of puberty and how babies are born, which, of course, happened some years ago. Not even healthy versus toxic relationships. No, nothing most parents must face. This one was about death—her own—the timing and the promise of life that comes after. I needed to have *that* discussion. Though Sadie was well-versed in the latter, a straight discussion of assurance was vital.

I couldn't believe my turnaround. The ability to face the inevitable head-on. God's simple two words had given me courage, permission even to think it. I prayed he'd give me the words to share with Sadie.

By the early hours of the next morning, the discussion could wait no longer. It had been a grueling night. As one of the tumors was impacting Sadie's esophagus and swallowing wasn't happening effectively, I took to blending food combinations. Once Sadie'd had enough spoonfuls, she leaned back against her pile of favorite pillows, and a beam of sunrise poked through the blinds, adding a satisfying sort of buoyancy.

Now. I had to tell her now.

It was one of those life moments when you just want to run. Forget about everything… and maybe, just maybe, when you came back, all in the world would be right again. I planted myself on her bed, held her hands in mine. One of hers quite limp, given the weakness of her prosthetic arm, but the other still able to clasp mine in return. The look in her eyes was reminiscent of a double-edged sword, a shard of gray on one side, a glimmer of something shiny on the other.

"I think—I believe—honey, that God is calling you home." I clasped a tighter grip on her hands so she couldn't pull them away. My gaze steadied on her face.

Words hung in the little space between us. Haunting. Taunting. Was the devil himself laughing? Had he won?

She glared at me, an angry look, as though I were betraying her. Hope and trust in God that all would be well had always been our go-to.

"He wants… you back," I whispered.

Her head fell, trailing her gaze downward. She nodded, slow and deep. A single, supersized tear dropped, as if it'd been gathering, storing, and holding the wetness hostage for some time, its weight finally free to let go.

Somewhere, deep inside, Sadie had already known this.

I broke the long silence. "I can hardly blame him. I would too. I never want to let you go, be separated from you." I was crying inside, my tears mixing up good with the pool of blood left from yesterday's hack. It was amazing to watch my body hold it steady on the exterior. I wished so badly to change places with her.

Sadie's bottom lip quivered.

I tightened my grip on her hands.

"I don't know why, honey, but that's his plan. And, sweetheart, he loves you a thousand times more than I even could, and"—I pulled her chin up—"you know how much I love you."

She winced. Her left shoulder gave a slight rise and fall, the right still impaired by the limb-salvage surgery and the more recent protruding tumor.

"He'll keep you safe. You won't have cancer anymore. He adores you. I know it."

She nodded, knowing all this. A bittersweet concurrence.

"Don't tell anyone!" she cried.

She didn't want to disappoint anyone. Bless her. But I couldn't promise that. Calls had to be made.

As coincidence goes, our pastor, a lovely young woman whom Sadie knew and liked, was already scheduled to come for a visit that morning. Upon her arrival, the three of us prayed together.

We delivered the news to each of Sadie's closest family members, and each arrived later that day to spend time with her. Of course, there would be more family and plenty of friends we needed to arrange for visits. I planned to pull a schedule together for the coming few weeks, careful not to overburden Sadie's energy levels.

I amazed myself with how I'd been able to move into a mindset of preparation, a mode unthinkable less than twelve hours ago. But I'd heard those audible words last night—*"It's time."* Now, I had a new request of God.

*For starters, after the time comes, you must give me a signal when she gets there, so I know she is safe, home with you. I can't go with her, so please, please, make sure she doesn't get scared or confused. Have Jesus pick her up or at least someone reliable.*

Then I scoffed. Listen to me! *I'm sorry, God, I'm just being a mother. I know you'll get her back to you, safe.*

I hesitated, telling myself it was my knees struggling to come up to a stand. Reality was, I had a second request. I patted the cover on my bed as I debated, then went ahead with it.

*Secondly, God, if, in fact, this is real and you do take her, then you've got to take me too. Because I won't bear this. Perhaps give some weeks to pass for my family's sake.*

I knew this request was wrong, but what the hey, I didn't have the courage to face this loss. This was the only way I could think of to get through it—by knowing I'd be spared the pain. It was simple: I'd tie up loose ends and go with.

In my mind, that was the deal. I'd go along with this plan of his as long as he granted me those two simple requests. Let me know when she was safe with him and then, in good time—five months at the utmost—take me too.

It didn't take much to arrange a dinner so our family could be together. Being in a merged family, we always had at least two branches to think of. Most, including her dad, had already planned to come anyway to spend time with her. It gave my husband and me a chance to go and meet with a funeral planner to get the basics. Neither of us had gone through such a process before, so we were thankful that a family member was in the business.

Upon returning, I felt guilty. Sadie didn't know where we went or why. From her curious looks at me, she was suspicious as to where we'd gone. I'd betrayed her. I couldn't share where I went, not with several people about. I would, though, once we were alone. We had a pact. Plus, there was another six weeks or so, according to her doctor, so there'd be special times for the two of us to chat. I would find ways to discover her thoughts on all matters that lay ahead. She gave me a hug around my waist. Our eyes locked, hers in sadness.

I will never forget that I needed to attend to something in

the kitchen, a lasagna or some silly thing. We had a household, and hence, well, there were things to do, mouths to feed. I kissed her forehead.

Little did I realize that would be our last hug.

Before her dad left, he and my husband carried her, wheelchair and all, up the stairs. When did she get so weak she couldn't move from one chair to another? After everyone left, within the next hour, she had a hard time sucking in a breath. Her oxygen was already at its highest level. So I called our home care nurse, and even so late into the evening, she came straightaway.

Sadie's eyes were telling—she was scared. With nothing we could do to help her breathe, we called an ambulance. Sadie concurred. As much as she resisted emergency room visits, she wanted to go. She wasn't feeling safe with such inadequate oxygen. Tension was ballooning.

Two short and scrambled hours later, Sadie died.

## 27

It was a horrible passing. And the family members who made it to the emergency room witnessed it all. It left a stain on my soul. Like a blotch of dark ink absorbed into parchment, it could never be erased—

We weren't prepared for the DNR business, and the ER doctor naturally required some direction. A nurse, with gentle compassion, took me aside and explained that, if they resuscitated her, she would still have her cancer, we wouldn't be further ahead, and it wouldn't be doing our dear daughter any favors. We agreed to reject the ventilator, the decision spoken through a haze. We opted instead for increased oxygen support, swiftly put in place, holding time until her dad could arrive in another hour or so.

"Death was imminent." The words didn't register. The room froze.

When the medical attendants realized the child patient was actually eighteen, which meant she must be treated as an adult, our decision was reversed. A legal requirement, rightfully so. Yet instructions came with an urgency that left no room for calm. I was asked to speak with my daughter—urging that I tell her declining the ventilator would be the best choice.

A chilling cold crawled along my spine.

*No. No. No. No.*

The look in Sadie's eyes was something I shall never forget.

"What, Mama?" She'd caught a sense of the looming, thick tension. It was pretty tough to miss. Might she be thinking: No, Mama, I don't want to die?

*God. Where are you?! This is not fair. You cannot ask me to do this! I cannot tell her to choose death. No, God. Please! I beg you. Don't make me do this.*

A voice in the room pushed even harder. Her vitals weren't good. "Ask her." Sadie wasn't breathing, and neither was I. Even the room itself continued to hold its breath.

The attending nurse claimed, "No pulse, not getting a pulse."

Sadie just stared ahead.

We all watched with horror.

"She's gone," the ER doctor said. It was over. After a pause, he closed her eyelids and stepped away.

We just stood there as though we'd been unplugged from reality. Or plugged in. One or the other.

The tension from the medical urgency ceased.

Then her body made a big move.

Hope thumped my heart.

They had to be wrong. She was still with us.

But no. Apparently, an after-death exhale was a normal occurrence.

## 28

Like zombies, our family followed a nurse who guided us to gather in a small room. I was thankful for the scent of her kindness and empathy.

Then the nurse beckoned me. "Come." She took me to another small room where they'd moved Sadie's body. "Would you like to wash her?"

Of course. What a beautiful thing to offer a mother in such a scenario. I was so grateful.

A few nurses scurried and collected fragrant soaps for me and laid them on the window ledge. Then, at my urging, they left me with her alone.

"Hmm, which scent would you like, honey?" I whispered between shaky breaths.

We'd had eighteen months full of alone-time chats. This was just another, wasn't it? "Okay, honey. It's all over. You can sit up now."

*If only.*

I begged God: *Please, it can't be too late. Let it all be one big mistake. Won't you give her breath? Come on. You've done it before. Why won't you do it now? What about those healthy lungs and that new heart you gave her? Why then show me that!*

I diverted to the array of soaps. A tiny lavender bar was the one I chose. I let it soak in the blue plastic tub. A similar tub to the ones she'd been given many times to catch her stomach upheavals since chemotherapy started.

I studied her face, lovingly examined her skin, her peacefulness. I talked to her while wiping her forehead and her cheeks. I lifted her arms, a little frustrated that the pain pump was still a fixture disturbing the natural creation of her being.

Attempting to move one leg as it sat crooked and far apart from the other, I was taken aback by just how heavy it was. It could have been a bag of sand.

When I kissed her forehead, I jolted away, abandoning the idea that my daughter lay in front of me. So cold. Of course, she was cold. She was dead. That was a horrifying moment, coming to terms that she was no longer encased in that body.

Yet, also a freeing one.

I looked around the room, scouting for some kind of sign, then up toward the ceiling.

"Sadie?"

A nurse peeked into the room. "Just checking. You okay?"

I nodded, and she closed the door, leaving the two of us for a few more minutes.

"Are you here? Watching this. Can you hear me?" My breaths were uneven. "Is Jesus with you? Are you okay?"

She'd reached that mountaintop. I smiled for her.

What was she experiencing? Brilliance, warmth, freedom from a paining body? Love and joy beyond anything she'd ever known? Would she be just as shocked, trying to talk to me?

What if she were angry and screaming at me, "I thought you said I had six weeks!"

Did she think I lied to her?

I blew out a whole lot of air I hadn't realized I'd been holding captive.

"Bye, baby girl." The others wanted a few minutes with her too. I couldn't hog her. We'd only have a bit more time before the hospital needed the room back.

I stepped out and eventually left the hospital, feeling such betrayal. The action of going home without her… How could I just leave her behind?

# PART THREE

*The spiritual side of grief
is simply unresolved business
between God and the soul of the one not taken.*

# 29

**All the business** of death to deal with lay ahead. A tangled nest of wires occupied my head, a snarl of knots impossible to free, lest I grabbed hold of a loose end and pulled gently. As far as my heart goes? It fled. Disappeared. Went into hiding beneath a rock somewhere, afraid to come out. There were calls to break the news. Appointments to make—the pastor, the funeral home, the burial. Goodness, we didn't even have a cemetery in mind. And the service, or rather, a celebration of life. Yes, a celebration of life.

Of course, I didn't feel much like celebrating. Which hymns would Sadie like? Who would say what? How could we comfort our other children? What would help her school friends through this? And the absolute worst: which casket would be picked and which of her favorite outfits would we dress her in? None of the above had been given even an inkling of thought. Until now.

Our household got quite busy that morning as Sadie's friends awoke and read the news we wrote on her care blog. I loved how many of them came rushing over.

Various medical services called, wanting to pick up all the equipment we'd been using. "Seriously?" I ranted to my husband. "Couldn't they wait till after the funeral?" I hadn't had a chance to absorb her room as she left it.

But I understood. There'd be someone else, somebody's mother perhaps, who would appreciate the oxygen tank, IV pole, pain pump, or wheelchair sooner rather than later. I snapped a photo of all her equipment where Sadie last used it, knowing I'd need to process it later.

Silly.

So many people offered to do so many things, extending their help wherever needed. Though I didn't know what I needed, only that switching to autopilot was the way to get things done.

That was how I rolled.

Laughs between heart-arresting attacks filled the morning. Our home had often been somewhere for Sadie and her friends to meet. Though apparently, our house was also the party place when my husband and I were out of town, or so I learned that day. Such great stories as Sadie's friends reminisced, many BC (before cancer). The girls always cleaned up well because I had no idea. Hearing the stories brought momentary lightness, except tears flowed instead of party drinks today.

"So that's how my blender broke." I chuckled and hoped all their drinks were the girly mocktail sort.

Being a task-oriented, solution-focused thinker, I let my mind urge a change in direction. Plus, I needed an escape to breathe, to do something, to cross off a to-do on a scattered list.

I was already envisioning what I'd like for the funeral home, in particular, three identical picture frames. Don't ask me why. I just knew what I wanted. Likely because my head hurt too much to decide which single photo to use. The one with her happy face and long blondish hair prediagnosis? Or the one that proved just how beautiful she was with her bald head? Or the lovely photo that showed off her brunette curls, so soft and short, the 'do she sported during her final days? She had such a gorgeous smile all the time. No way would I ever be able to choose just one look. So, one of those simple wires I could pull out of my head was to find and purchase three identical frames. I was determined to get that job done, even if I wasn't in a stable state of mind.

I knew just where to go—the photo shop with a wall full of frames at our local outdoor mall mere miles away. In the parking lot, I slumped over the steering wheel. Had she really left us last night? It was just past midnight, so technically, today was the day of her passing.

Sadie died today.

I steadied my breathing—

Into the shop, I entered. No one would have an inkling as to how I felt, paralyzed, attempting to be normal, albeit numb. I strolled along, observing the selection of frames. Why did nothing suit? I rattled several around on a shelf. My distress must have shown, for a saleslady approached with a placid, "Can I help you?"

I set down the ones I'd gathered to get them out of the way. "I'm looking for an identical set of three eight-by-tens—a modern style preferably, three matching ones."

"Oh." She balanced a frame I'd placed too close to the edge. "I'm sorry, but our stock is all one-offs. But many of our customers like these series frames.…"

She kept talking, but I wasn't listening. Her name tag revealed she was the store's manager. "Really?" I admit, it was an insulting sneer. I gave her my best condescending face, the one I inherited from my father. "You don't carry three of anything. This *is* a frame shop, is it not?"

She took it personally, bit her lower lip, and walked away. I was stuck on getting three identical, single frames. Once something like that was in my head, that's it. Nothing else would do.

No mismatch of frames for my Sadie, and the frames must be the stand-alone type, not attached as though dependent on the other. I left the store in a huff.

Deeply discouraged as though the world had just ended, I dogged my way back to my car. An inkling twitched at me, encouraging a turnaround.

*Go back.*

I ignored it.

I sat in my car and stared at nothing, simply needing a moment.

"No, Mama, that store," I heard in my head.

"Sadie?"

I looked at the empty passenger seat. "Honey, you're here?"

I gave my head a shake.

Then I heard it again, "There."

Was it—was *she*—directing me to go back and look again?

"There's nothing there," I whispered.

Maybe I was truly sane. And if I wasn't, hey, that's okay. My daughter just died. Give me a break.

"Go back," the voice was gentle, female, and empathetic, like a mature, all-knowing Sadie, my Sadie in a different form. She directed me to try again, to go find those three frames. She was adamant. "There!"

*Yup, bossy. It's gotta be my Sadie.*

I eyed the photo shop. Seriously, I did not want to go back in there. I did happen to show my disappointment with them not having any three-of-a-kind frames. Sadly, it wasn't a fine moment when I handed over some of my frustration to its manager. Clearly not my norm.

"No. There."

"The drug store?"

Elated by the concept of Sadie giving me direction, I got out of the car and walked to the drug store. "Coming with?" I choked. No response. I turned to head back to my car, shaking off the silly experience.

"Go. Get them!" her voice again spoke in my head.

I hurried into the drug store, which had a gift section. In fact, the store had more gifts than anything else. I strolled the row of shelves. Picture frames were scattered throughout the shop. Certainly not the diverse collection offered in the photo shop next door, but they did have one suitable frame. Of course, there was just one.

I stood there. *Now what?*

The sales attendant had been watching me as though she were suspicious. Perhaps the photo shop manager next door warned her about me.

What did she think? I was planning to put three eight-by-ten picture frames down my pants? I held the one up. "Any chance you have more just like this?"

She shook her head and went about other business in the shop, leaving me to wander again as if I were a sane, casual shopper. But if I wasn't imagining things, Sadie had directed me into this shop. Must be that salesclerk had something.

I revisited the shelves. Perhaps I missed something.

Aha, I did. I found a similar frame tucked in behind a bunch of graduation knickknacks. A reminder: she wouldn't graduate from high school.

No. I wasn't letting that thought bring me down, not here, not now. Be happy. There was a frame identical to the one I liked. That was something. I picked it up, clasping two frames to my chest.

"You sure you don't have another one of these?" I asked.

"We never order three of the same."

I hugged the frames tighter, unwilling to give up on my Sadie-directed quest.

The woman's expression softened. Perhaps reading my desperation, she looked around the shop. No one, besides me. "I can go back into the storage room to check. Maybe there's something similar from last season."

That probably wasn't something she would typically do when only one person was minding the place.

Then she came back, holding out a dusty box with an identical frame inside. "Wow, you're in luck." She waved it. "Almost didn't see it."

A deep flip-flop thrashed inside my chest. *Sadie, I can't believe this.*

I felt renewed. My girl was alive and well, just no longer in her cancer-racked body. The fact that I was leaving with three identical frames from a store she urged me to go into was proof enough for me.

Back into the car, I spoke to her. "Kiddo, that was amazing!"

But there was no response or further chitchat.

My mood upon arriving home was considerably better. Could I tell anyone about my experience? Better not. They'd fetch a white jacket and wrap me up. Plus, who loses a child and goes shopping the same day?

I ran up the stairs and into my room. Did that really just happen? That sensation of Sadie's presence beside me had slipped away. Had she left to visit another family member or one of her many dear friends? Knowing her, she would do her best to spread her giggly, bossy self around. I love her.

"Thank you, sweetie," I whispered. "Thank you, Jesus, for letting her speak to me, for allowing me to hear her." That was not a normal, typical thing. 'Least as far as I figured anyway. How many other parents who lost a child experienced such and, for obvious reasons, kept quiet about it?

I confirmed to myself then and there not to broadcast my experience. Though temptation ached to blurt it out, particularly whenever anyone advised me that she now rested in peace.

*Nah. She's alive, not sleeping like dust.*

I was already a bit of a spectacle to others—that woman who was so confident in God that she believed a miracle would come and her child would live.

Well, guess what. She did!

## 30

**Though most referred** to it as a Celebration of Life, for me, it was a ceremony. I was releasing my child symbolically into the arms of God. Of course, she was always his in the first place. Not to mention, she was already there—yes, I was confident in that. It was the closing of a chapter in a book, a story that continued. Even so, it was crushing to read the pages that came next, much less turn them.

Every day was so very long. I took time off work but spent most of it alone. I hadn't a clue what to do with myself. My whole life's purpose in the last eighteen months had surrounded Sadie. Our favorite thing to do was plan for fun things to look forward to, then count down the days to whatever that something special and unrelated to cancer was.

Now, like a ghost in my house, I wandered from room to room, and I had no energy to change anything. Had it all somehow been my fault? Why couldn't everything be as it was when she was alive and with us, before cancer?

Despite the gray, wet spring, I coaxed myself to get out. Just take a drive. Mindless aiming, I had no need to run an errand. Except that morning for picture frames and her visitations and funeral, I refused to go anywhere. I couldn't even bear to enter a grocery store. That would suggest things were normal. And make no mistake, they were not. Thankfully, my husband did the food shopping for a while.

The car in motion, something aroused my senses as I drove. I wasn't alone. I hadn't heard from Sadie since that morning she passed, though I craved her presence. Still, this was different. An unmistakable hand appeared, pointing a finger to make a turn. Translucent and vague, not dissimilar to the degree of visibility of those beings who brought Sadie new lungs and a heart that night.

A new body. Wherever she was, she had a new body.

"Okay, where are we going?" I asked this ethereal gesturer while placing my blinker to prepare for the suggested turn.

Such utterly unusual oddities came so naturally now. I hadn't the energy even to doubt what I saw. It was not a hand that belonged to Sadie, as it was a broad palm with a thick wrist. Masculine and notably well-manicured.

"Sadie?" I asked anyway. No response, though it felt right. Comforting. *Just go with it. Follow.*

The suggestive signaling continued as I, rather we, made a number of turns, heading north of the city and finally east-bound onto a country road. I hadn't planned on such a trip. Late afternoon meant the city's traffic got busy, and I'd do anything to avoid that time of day. But I followed the gentle hand and its directive motions. Across the top of the city, we went, then past a large and popular outdoor market.

I gazed upon the empty lot. It appeared so sad in the weeping drizzle.

"Keep going." Quiet words played inside my head, and so I did.

When the hand signaled to enter a Walmart parking lot, I thought for sure my overactive mind was playing tricks. Just a silly grieving woman. "I don't need anything here," I spoke aloud. If some kind of presence were there in my car, they would have been assaulted by the anger in my voice. "Why on earth did you direct me to Walmart! I am *not* going in."

I slammed the car into park out of frustration.

And there it was.

Beyond the parking lot, on the distant horizon, a large rainbow arched from one side of the country landscape to the other. A full arch.

"God's promise." The words slipped off my lips. I burst into tears. Uncontrollable sobs, actually. I must have sat there for thirty minutes. Blinking and wiping away wetness from dripping eyes.

My heart sank so deep I was sure my digestive system was squeezing it like a piece of meat. I managed a muffled thank you, though the hand had long been gone.

It was the deepest and most satisfying sob I'd had yet.

Then grayness fell, and the rainbow faded.

I drove home with slow-moving rush-hour traffic, working hard to pay attention to all the stops and starts on the expressway.

That magical happening did much to pick my soul back up to a higher level of thinking where it belonged. At least for a little while. It seemed to be a game of rise and fall.

# 31

THAT BEAST OF grief would not leave me alone. Rather, he attacked with vigor. Vicious and unrelenting. I succumbed numerous times, pushing me into knee-dropping wails.

It had been weeks since the rainbow. God, his messengers, and Sadie had all gone silent. Too busy or what?

I left the top of that mountain cloaked in abandonment. That glorious otherworldly place was silent and unreachable now. My descent a suffering cold with haunting winds. My purpose finished, my soul discarded. I tossed my Bible into an imagined chasm. It smacked a wall. Pages crumpled as it rested on my bedroom floor.

*Sorry, God. This is becoming a habit.*

I didn't stop believing in God. I just didn't like him so much. An explanation as to why he had to take Sadie was what I wanted. I'd surely earned at least that. And if he did start talking again, I needed to understand why he made a game of it too.

My husband thought it best to get me away. Perhaps he thought I was certifiably insane.

We took a twenty-four-hour drive to South Beach in Miami. Then he left me inside a rented condo alone so he could find a video store. The next series of *Lost* or something intense, to keep our minds occupied. Though sunny and warm outside, I preferred the comfy inside with the curtains drawn.

I let the swirl in my head loosen up. I named off each of our sarcoma patient friends and their families we'd met along the way, all in my heart. Infuriatingly, there were far more deaths in our local region than the official sarcoma statistics quoted for the entire country. The numbers were absurdly inaccurate.

Sadie had banged her right shoulder harshly when she was eleven. Did that have something to cause her bone to grow unnecessary bone matter? She'd also had a hepatitis injection in her right shoulder, given she'd been exposed at a childcare facility. Did that have some type of long-game effect? Her early years were spent in a city where fluoride was incorporated into the water. Could that have been the cause? Did we have abnormal genes in our ancestry that we weren't aware of? Were there environmental toxins in our home? Was it the foods we ate, the mice in the wheat fields that eventually churn into the flour I buy? Did we ever live beneath or close by hydro or other such towers?

Why were there no surveys taken from patients? Such a missed opportunity for a collected intelligence bank was better than doing nothing. I couldn't understand why, in this day and age, the treatment for osteosarcoma still felt so archaic. The same regimen had been in place for decades. With survival rates discouraging and research advances seemingly so limited, this form of cancer will continue to set its eyes on youth, circling as a vulture looking for its next meal.

Easy to dismiss all inquisitions, they covered up what I'd been afraid of. Had it been something spiritual? With all the visions and dreams in my life, how could I deny it? An invisible enemy was out there. Ever since I could remember.

I stepped onto the back patio for fresh air when a rustling of bushes behind me interrupted my pity party. A distinguishing, strong notion of her presence.

"Sadie?" I whispered.

"Yes, Mama."

*Hah, yes!* My heart fleeted with excitement. "You okay?"

"Of course!"

"Where are you?"

"Heaven."

"Do you like it there?" Dumb question, but I had to ask.

"Oh my, yes!"

Her enthusiasm settled the uneasiness I'd allowed to build in my chest, all due to an overactive mindset. "I don't know what to ask you." And I honestly didn't at the time.

"That's okay." Her voice came soft in my head.

"I love you." Following my words, her infectious smile flooded my mind, erasing all the silly anger. "Is this real? Sadie, am I really having a conversation with you?"

"Don't be afraid," she said.

"Okay." I paused. "What should I do now?" I felt so lost inside myself, within this world. So out of any sense of belonging.

"Just wait, Mama. It'll come."

"You were a gift to me."

"I know," she said. "Enjoy your picnic. Gotta go."

"Picnic?" I queried. What picnic?

Just then, my husband's key clicked to unlock the condo's front door. He was home from the video store and brought with him pizza, snacks, and drinks to accompany our binge-watch.

## 32

THAT BEAST WAS tenacious. The poison it employed granted tremendous success—unyielding grief. Even so, I had more in my resource kit these days to protect myself.

The battle was on.

And I fought back.

Sadie lived. I embraced envisioning her hanging out with Jesus, going about, exploring the heavens, taking time out to spy on those below. The cute and effective way she bossed anyone into anything with that sweet, pleading face. Jesus had his hands full! Yes. Sadie was just fine.

It was me, myself, that darkness gripped. The ferocious black tail of that tornado tugged nonstop, coaxing me into its deadly grind of self-condemnation. This storm hoisting me to wherever didn't appear ready to calm anytime soon. The only difference was that I was on my own now. A void where time didn't click and fog didn't lift. Motivation to fight for myself, however, wavered in want and purpose. I hoped God hadn't forgotten our five-month deal. I just needed to get to that milestone. Then I, too, could be free.

Friends practically tossed grief books at my feet every week, a library shelf full of them. I refused to crack open the covers. How was it another human could know how *I* felt, what *I* grappled with, how so very much *I* missed my daughter, much less provide a written prescription to map my way out of the grinding swirl? I whispered apologies to all the goodness my friends had shown, keeping it quiet that the local thrift shop was thankful for the book donations.

Still, the storm howled for my surrender, and my soul searched for ways to survive it.

Thankful for the warmth of my car heater, I waited for my son to finish a music lesson. It was cold, dark, and rainy, not typical early May weather. Straightening my back, I declared what I'd heard in church many times before. This time, rather than repeating it mechanically, dang it, I meant it.

"Seek first the kingdom of God."

That's what I'd lean into, a way to prioritize. From this moment forward, that would be my number one goal. "Then all the rest will follow." I would count on that promise. That would be my way to hang on through this maelstrom, keep myself from drowning. If I kept at it, maybe all those tangled-up wires in my head would come undone, and I could pull them out effortlessly and toss them away. It was a hopeful plan, something to hang onto.

I'd look it up, read the verse when I got home, just to be sure I had it right.

It was an easy declaration. God's kingdom was where my Sadie lived, and that was where I wanted to be. Sooner or later, anyway. Exactly when would depend on God.

Not more than a few weeks later, a vision came. Visions that once fed me frequently now rarely appeared, at least nothing like the intensity of Sadie's final six months. Why the hiatus when I really needed that connection?

But then, there he was.

Jesus.

*Finally, some visual communication again.*

At the end of a path. Trees behind him, a forest of such. To his left, an opening to a cave, a large rock aside it. He sat on the boulder. His eyes locked a glazing beam into mine. His invitation came without words. I could enter the cave now, if I wanted.

This caused me to pause. Sadie had already entered. She was deep inside. An entrance perhaps she had passed through, a tomb of sorts leading to the beyond.

Wasn't this what I prayed for? Perhaps demanded even. If God were to take Sadie, then he'd have to take me too. Otherwise, I'd never have surrendered to this plan of his.

"All rest will follow" played in my mind.

So now what? Should I enter? Was this where and when all such "rest" followed? No more weariness from the thoughts in my head. Or destructive lava heaving from the floorboards of my heart.

His right hand made a gentle movement. Come. Enter.

Was it a dare?

I didn't want him to sense my hesitation, and I realized that I, too, was sitting on a rock. Why was I not getting up to enter the cave? It seemed a no-brainer. I could be with Sadie. My heartache would cease. If I entered, there was no coming back out.

I watch him watching my expressions. Assessing my reaction, I bet. Likely wondering what held me back. Of course, I knew instantly. My husband, my other children, my parents. Still, something more, I couldn't label it.

He reached with one hand to catch my head as it drooped from foolishness. With his other hand, he closed my eyelids.

I knew then what I needed next. To be still. Lean on him and soak in that calming peace, the kind only he could provide.

The vision gone, my mood lifted. My harbored feelings of rejection, I cast away. In came the knowing that I would go home one day too, only when the timing was right. And sitting on the couch in my heart-room, I knew full well, I couldn't dare leave my family. Nor did I want to! So, I wouldn't be so irrational. So selfish.

For once, even the coffee I let grow cold slipped down my throat suitably well. Normally, that would have been quite distasteful.

That invitation to enter that cave wasn't going away. But Jesus showed me to myself, called my bluff if you will. The recall of a prior year's vision of that same cave inspired a chuckle. That the opening was the entrance to our Creator's nostril—a way into his being, simply through an intake of breath. He sucked us back. Like sweet, pleasing incense. One would never hear that at church: "Thou shalt enter through the nostril of God." Just imagine the perplexed faces of those in the pews!

So, if I was going to be around for a while, I need a plan. I couldn't remain still, not just yet. Not when my head was full of chaos in desperate need of categorizing. I'd make a list. Then, perhaps, choose which to focus on and prioritize.

Such structure could only be helpful. It might even unravel some wires from that snarly nest in my head. In no particular order, using my journal diary, I jotted what plagued me—

ANGRY. Accurate information on sarcoma cancer was impossible to find. Evening after evening, I scoured reputable sites, digging deep into statistics. The numbers I came across seemed inconsistent, especially when it came to how many teens and young adults had been diagnosed—perhaps even misdiagnosed—with sarcomas. To me, this was scandalous, an insult to youth, saying what? They didn't matter? This was 2009, and things needed to change.

*Breathe.*

DISCOURAGED. On the topic of finances, I must get back to work. Bills were piling up.

Why did we have to live in a world that revolved around money?

FRUSTRATED. I couldn't seem to let go of the words from one obstinate woman who addressed me sternly in front of Sadie, accusing me of being in denial. She encouraged our acceptance into a program in her brochure, a different path—a step-by-step way to the grave. At the time, Sadie was still receiving chemotherapy, and applications had been made for clinical trials. It wasn't time to "switch gears" as she suggested. I had asked her to leave our home, but her accusation lingered in my head. I wasn't in denial.

Was I wrong? No, I wasn't wrong. I chose faith even when all the facts were on the table, and I'd never regret that.

Still, I could have prepared Sadie better.

Reflection allowed me to yank a good chunk of that wire out. I admitted I'd work on the forgiveness part, but later.

This was becoming an intense list. *Keep going, just make more coffee.*

DEATH ITSELF. This would be a favorite debate I'd welcome. It wasn't life and death, I decided. Rather, it's life and life. I would gleefully give this topic heavy doses of my attention. Definitely worth spending time on.

DOUBTING. Should I have incorporated more natural remedies? Rumors swirled that some patients did, even when given explicit advice not to. We trusted our oncologist and didn't question him, didn't want to interfere with the treatments. Still, I wondered.

I placed this topic on a low priority. If I discovered we took a wrong path treatment-wise, it would only further darken my doorstep.

A ding intruded. Clothes in the dryer were done. *Never mind. Keep trudging forward with this list. It'll help.*

BITTER. The big why? Why hadn't I been tuned into this oxycodone drug fiasco until now? Why, when a national emergency over this addictive drug surfaced, and yet, Sadie was prescribed generous volumes? Now looking back, I wondered: was her anxiety from needing another dose, or was it truly from pain? More than likely, some combination of both.

Flashes of Sadie in pain churned my stomach. It helped her. A saving grace. So, let it go, let it go, let it go!

UNREST. My prayer content. Had I prayed incorrectly? Did I not lay out our hearts and explain ourselves well enough? Was I not earnest enough? Was I a sinner in God's eyes and not worth listening to?

*Stop it! Move on.*

HAUNTING PAST. Then there's the axman Jake. Remember him? That haunting visitation. Was he the jealous man who powered a hatchet through my great-grandfather's arm, shoulder blade, and heart? Hmm, same places where tumors invaded Sadie's body. Should I acknowledge this? A passed-on curse or a super weird coincidence?

Unsettling, I couldn't wrap my head around that one. Too weird.

I leaned back, closed my eyes. Oh my, how much more circulated in this head of mine? A memory floated into the front of line position. How could I have forgotten it? "God, I'm so sorry. You did warn me. And I shoved you under the carpet."

That time, seven years before Sadie's diagnosis, he had pointed three spaces to my right, and a child sprang with excitement and ran to Jesus. Then those two walked away without as much as a glance back.

My wrist shook as I jotted down my final heading. AMAZEMENT.

The unseen meant business. No doubt about that. Was it my punishment? Or perhaps a forewarning so I could be prepared? Whatever battle God was fighting, whatever message he was sending, I needed to figure that out.

Face it, that one had to be my priority.

## 33

THERE SHE WAS.

Buoyant and exhilarated. Jumping up and down impatiently. She positioned a forefinger as though to begin a count. One.

One of what?

Then a second finger. Her excited leaps continued, and I couldn't help but laugh at the joy of seeing my daughter so full of gladness. Her skin and energy a vision of perfect health. My heart in dire want to burst.

I wasn't going to jinx this vision, no pinching self. Just enjoy! Don't waste this with tears.

Sadie was right there, in the upper corner of my bedroom. The scene couldn't have felt any more normal, in the yes-this-is-real sense.

*There you are! It's about time you showed up!*

And there she was. Grinning triumphantly with three fingers flashing. Pulsing straight at me. A distinct message of sorts.

I wanted to grab them and pull her out of that transparent image and right back into my world, the physical one.

But she was in the utmost glorious place for humankind, so why ruin things for her?

There were no spoken words, just squeals of laughter, silent, yet the delight bubbled and bounced off the walls. Reaching behind her back, she pulled out a gift box, tied with a bow, and cupped in her hands. Both her arms stretched my way. Her face beamed.

"Thank you, honey," I said. The whole scene surprisingly natural, as though it were just another birthday and she had never died. But even the seriously focused life-sustaining organs inside my body took time out to smile, if that were possible.

I was in heavenly awe.

What gift could she possibly give me? How could she give me something across this divide? Of course, it's God's veil, so he could do as he pleased with it. Close it, open it, or make it thick and black or thin and see-through.

Again, her upheld hand pumped that three-finger clutch. Whatever was inside that gift box, there were three of them.

My arms wanted to embrace her. Of course, I knew I couldn't hold her. Instead, they reached openly to imagine myself receiving the box. Surprised by my calm excitedness, I asked her, "What's in it?"

*For you!* Her motions spoke the words. Somehow, she had arranged a gift for me.

*You always were so determined and still are!* "How do I... actually get it?"

She just jumped excitedly some more, then disappeared.

I took a seat on my bed and stared at the empty ceiling corner. Without a doubt, I'd just seen her, my child. Very much happy, very much still *her*. The whole of me grinned with sensational contentedness.

*So natural, so wonderfully normal.* Reality was taking on an entirely new meaning.

Three somethings in that gift box of hers? Was it a message of the Trinity? It seemed more of a material gift of some sort. I chuckled. That's my girl. Still shopping. I imagined the pleading and begging she gave someone so she could come to me like that!

All morning, most of that week in fact, I relished her visit. Seeing her so happy. And on top of that, wanting to gift me something. Something I could never receive—we were on different realms, after all. That didn't matter. The darkness in my heart gave way to light. She was alive. Even more proof had come. I had full belief she lived, and she was happy. And with such joy, that was a moment in my life I shall never forget!

I no longer had a simple hope for eternity. Rather, I now relished a strong belief of knowing.

It seemed a well-accepted thing that God sent prophetic dreams for reasons to protect and warn. Though I wondered just how normal it was for God to let children in heaven come to see and chat with their parents on earth—and give gifts no less. I had a fairly strong notion that was not so normal, and it was far too real for me to believe my mind was playing tricks. It couldn't be a memory recall. Sadie was wearing the cutest jumper, a style of clothing she'd never worn before. And her face had beamed with a whole new, fresh appearance.

I settled it. It was real, had to be. It was a genuine encounter, a gift from God.

I smiled. Perhaps he was easing my sorrow. Validation shot down the stubborn niggling in my heart that God had been punishing me. I chose to accept the accompanying blessing of affirmation.

Despite the wonderful encounter, that beast of grief clutched its way back, squarely atop my shoulders in a matter of days. Though its weight had shifted somewhat, it kicked and poked even more viciously, attempting to maintain its ideal position to push me down, preferably to keep me there. Shaking it off seemed impossible.

Unlike being "down in the dumps" as my mother might refer to or termed as "profuse sadness," this was a far different feeling. A brutal wrestling. A crushing yoke with a dark mission. Was this a taste of what people diagnosed with a serious depression disorder must deal with? I shuddered and gained a deeper respect for those who push through their lives with such an unseen torment upon their shoulders.

## 34

A DEAR GIRLFRIEND of mine offered to take me away for a few days, choosing a modest resort in Arizona, to a place claiming to be known for its healing powers. Once we arrived, pursuing the local activities guide, I was excited to learn that one of the top dream interpreters who focused on biblical explanations just happened to be in town.

Coincidence? How could it be? I hadn't shared much of my keen interest in the meaning of dreams. And here I was, in the same location and at the same time as a well-known expert in the field, at least according to my online sleuthing fetish. Completely unplanned.

I showed up to the man's service. Excited chatter rose from a long lineup wrapped around the building of the hosting church. Keep an open mind, I warned myself. It's okay to let that guard down a little. At least I wasn't sneaking into a side door in the dark of night. The remembrance caused a bittersweet chuckle that wrapped a blanket of warmth around my shoulders.

Once inside, I felt oddly out of place, so I took a chair in an empty back row. Everyone else scrambled to get as close to the front as possible. A traditional Lutheran, I wasn't used to Pentecostal-style worship.

A good half hour of upbeat worship songs followed. Several I knew, as they had been Sadie's favorites. I sang along and tapped my feet. But mostly I watched in awe as the entire assembly waved their arms, jumped up and down, and even cried. Why couldn't I partake, be less conservative? I just couldn't. So I had to rest in knowing God knew how I felt inside. Then I prayed fervently, asking him to allow blessings of joy to come upon me, to lift me out of my darkness.

The keynote speaker delved into his experiences, countless prophetic visions, and how his mother was forewarned of her soon-to-be-born son's abilities. He highlighted God's warning that globally, in every way imaginable, we were heading for major upheaval. That God was calling on his people to enter deepened spiritual awareness, so they'd learn to trust and rely on him once such turbulence hit.

His focus on Romans 4 underscored the power of faith. We couldn't do anything to make ourselves right with God, so it was all about who we trusted. We needed to trust God. The God of the heavens, none other, could get you there. The world had entered a phase when God was pouring out blessings of increased spiritual capacity to encourage believers to deepen their relationship with him. Like children, we needed to learn and build our trust so that, when such turbulence hit, we were mature in our faith.

It made more sense than anything else I'd read or heard on a Sunday morning. Any haunting concerns that a vivid imagination took a seat at the reality table or that I was silly in choosing faith in what appeared to others as denial, I could now abandon. I hoped God looked upon me favorably for sticking firm to hope right up to the moment he whispered, "It's time."

*I did the right thing.*

Only—did this suggest I'd been in training up to this point? Was God preparing me for this terrible turbulence that was yet to come?

At a minimum, I left with a greater sense of belonging. Many others, it seemed, were recipients of God's divine interactions. Such were not as foreign as I once thought. I needn't feel alone. And to many in the assembly, it was no concern if they hadn't had special dreams or visions. A strong faith without this "proof" meant even more.

"Then Jesus told him, 'Because you have seen me, you have believed; blessed are those who have not seen and yet have believed'" (John 20:29). Yes, I took that verse as a gentle rebuke.

I guess God had to bonk me over the head to force a change. If he hadn't done so, I'm not sure my faith would have sprouted to where it is right now.

## 35

Following the Arizona visit, a whole new course of visions kicked off, like a television murder-mystery series. It wasn't from a state of mental calm. My mind still had a lot of clearing out to do. As did my heart-home. Some emotions were just plain stubborn. I chalked up the visions to the deep spiritual hunger consuming me. I wanted answers from God. The cold, hard truth. Life wasn't fun and games. There was a lurking seriousness that needed uplifting. Even so, I wasn't prepared for what came my way—

A floating casket, the front end open, the back end closed. Dark-brown in color. Light streamed from the lifted flap, so much so that the brilliance hid the body inside. Presuming, that is, one was in there. Intrinsically, I knew that casket was, or would be, mine. Suspended in midair, its message hung, waiting to be realized.

The last time I saw something similar, I'd learned of a terrible accident that took a young life. Did this mean my death was coming?

*Hey, God? I kinda thought that old deal of ours had been squashed?*

The next day, I watched a murder. Mine!

When I awakened, another scene took up most of the room, like I was in a movie theater's front row, sans popcorn. I saw myself right in the center of it all. The on-screen version of me leaned back, lying in position on a bed of picture-perfect grass. It could have been a romance feel-good movie. There I was, resting in the presence of Jesus on one side of me, Sadie on the other. A lovely day surrounded us, a parklike setting, bright-blue sky, lush and shady trees, a calm, peaceful feeling.

Without so much as an orchestra to dive into wary notes that would send off a screaming siren, an unanticipated dagger appeared. Sharp and bloodthirsty. The blade raised itself. No hands clasped to its handle. It hung high.

I felt my breath pile up and halt like a water dam when its gates are sealed tight. Was I the only one to sense the danger?

The blade thrust down, a violent jab direct into that heart of mine. Sadie gasped and placed her hands over her mouth, her concerned expression devastating. She'd had no idea this was going to happen. Of course, nor did I.

All the while, Jesus remained calm. He must've expected this action. Not only was it no surprise to him, but he also did nothing to stop it. Nor anything to calm poor Sadie. Never mind offering any consolation to my now-dead corpse, either.

Without hands on the dagger, I couldn't know who was responsible. What a torment watching Sadie's face. Seeing how she must have felt to witness something so terrible.

Another trick? This stuff always meant something. It just took some thinking to figure it out.

I let my primary response run its course of emotions. Just when I had stepped up my trust, God went and pulled a stunt like that. I thought it, but didn't dare say it. And Jesus—he just sat there as my chest was stabbed. What bothered me most was Sadie's gasp and expression, her body numb and reeling.

I was out of my element, once again.

Eventually, I pushed myself to call a spade a spade. I knew

well by now that secondary thinking was critical, such with analytical reasoning. There had to be a key message God wanted me to take away from this.

"For whoever wants to save their life will lose it, but whoever loses their life for me will find it" (Matthew 16:25).

Had I just lost mine? This, the cost of coming to know Jesus.

My knowledge of biblical messages may have been limited to page flipping and sermons while in the pew, but this was one I easily recalled. The concept of dying so that Christ might live within you, take up permanent residence in one's heart-home, was rawness rooted in poetry. This must be it. My old life dies; my new one, with him, lives. This was one of those recurring themes in the New Testament: the true sense of *knowing* Christ.

*If I had known you were going to move in, Jesus, I would've bought a new couch.*

I committed to read the Bible front to back, starting first thing the next morning, assured there'd be even more answers waiting for me to discover. Besides, I wanted to be better prepared for what could come next. Reading his Word was the least I could do. Having come to that conclusion, I was eager to get going.

## 36

Though that needle of faith moved a significant degree, an unshakable blackness continued to dwell inside me. A stricken grief anchored itself around my ankles, chaining its prisoner while dreadful waves of defeat washed over me.

Upon waking each day, I asked for joy. That it might flood my heart, bring a much-needed lightness to my lungs, my breath. *Please,* I begged. Another day needed to be faced.

Eventually, a renewal of energy came with an enlightening dream—

A timeworn woman cloaked in somber black bent at her waist, examining broken bits scattered around her weathered flat and leathery boots. Something, a meager structure, had once stood around her. A house had just blown up. Or something smashed into it. Either way, it didn't matter. She was standing in the ruins of what was once her home.

I couldn't ignore the dull thump in my chest, the empathy for the woman. It seemed she'd misunderstood the protection of her shelter—positive she was safe from the storm. But now, she stood amongst the devastation. She'd lost everything. And she appeared so old, how could she start over? Rebuild? The woman's lips didn't move, but I wished I knew her thoughts.

She lowered further and reached for a piece on the ground, a remnant she'd been eyeing. Careful not to touch the sharp edges, she clasped it with both hands and straightened her body, holding the fragment high against the after-storm blue sky. She studied its triangular shape as though it had meaning, some kind of piece to move forward with. Just as curiosity struck me, the scene disappeared.

I connected to that spiritual epiphany.

For starters, that woman was me. Horrifying, if that was truly how God saw me, a wretched soul. Did anyone really think about what their soul looked like? It meant facing many truths. Yet there I be, the old version, the one he would redeem, not condemn. The one who died by dagger, buried in that casket. The one whose house was smashed to bits when that storm slapped the earth.

I shouldn't be so happy I recognized it so quickly. It was quite… pathetic. Sorrowful. True.

So now what?

Out of the brokenness, a piece the shape of a triangle. The moving scene focused on that, its final ending credits. Goodness, the Trinity! This was God confirming the three parts of himself.

He had already shown me how his Son, Jesus, was missing from my life. And now, he was bringing the Holy Spirit into the fold.

The divine threesome was always preached and talked about. I'd never really taken up the notion that God's Spirit was, in fact, an entity in itself. The three together made up God. I'd read that in John 14:16–17a where Jesus is quoted, "'And I will ask the Father, and he will give you another Helper, to be with you forever—the Spirit of truth'…" And also, John 16:13, "But when he, the Spirit of truth, comes, he will guide you into all the truth. He will not speak on his own; he will speak only what he hears, and he will tell you what is yet to come."

Like part 2 of my dagger-to-death escapade came this scene next—a helper for the rest of the transition. So then, the next foundation I built would be one of truth. A heart-home impervious to future storms as long as I let Christ take the lead and I followed the wisdom of God's Spirit.

A sarcastic accusation hurled its way to the interior of my stomach and gnawed at the lining.

It took Sadie's passing for me to give God more than ceremonial due?

"Wretched man that I am!" (Romans 7:24).

## 37

The five-month milestone felt worse than the day it happened. Though numbing subsided, the wound of grief was still open and weeping. I wasn't prepared to remove the bandaging for others to see, and the real world wasn't exactly an ointment of infection protection. So many new layers of skin needed to form, lest the longing and sadness for all things that would never be would only stir abrasively and prolong healing.

There was her high school graduation. Although knowing Sadie, her prom would have been more important. A college acceptance letter and planning out her first year of postsecondary school, perhaps. An engagement ring on her finger one day? Oh my, a wedding even and, just imagine, grandchildren! Watching Sadie with her own family.

That was the life my girl wanted. In grade eight, for career day, she followed a stay-at-home mom. "That's all I want when I grow up," she had stated with defiance. "My dream life is a family to take care of." Plus, of course, "I like to shop, so my husband needs to be rich." That was our Sadie, forever grinning with a mischievous delight.

But our Sadie wasn't coming back. And Scripture readings couldn't change that.

I read of recent some Old Testament taunts when God took a child as punishment for sin, even the beloved King David wasn't spared. Of course, he had an affair, then had the woman's husband killed. All I did was be confused, foolish, and not truly know God's Son until he chucked me to his feet.

Then I'd also read many confirmations from the New Testament, stating that one who did not believe in God's Son couldn't claim to know God. So did I correct my sin too late? If God knew my future, why would he not spare us such sorrow?

Still, I often refused to use the word *death* or acknowledge that Sadie *died*. No, Sadie simply *passed* to a new world, from one realm to another. She hadn't experienced a true death, just a passing through that veil.

Common sense hadn't a chance to prevail this day. I chose to believe the sovereign God had rejected me. This five-month anniversary of Sadie's passing was a day of emotional opposites meeting head-on.

I opened the cupboard. *That* cupboard. The one still full of Sadie's medications. No one ever came to collect the ample leftovers, at least a dozen containers half full of prescribed tablets, pills, and liquids. Most for pain. Most addictive. All deadly. Potentially.

*Quickly and quietly with no fuss.*

The deal I'd made with God, then taken back, waved an ugly rising in my chest. That original deal, the five-month marker to end my pain, perhaps, would have been a better solution.

An echo haunted: God wanted Sadie; he didn't want me.

Mechanically, my arm reached for the tray. I counted seven containers of oxycodone, anywhere from twenty to fifty tablets in each. I snorted. "I bet this could cover a few mortgage payments."

My fingers thickened as I opened each one and dumped them in a pile, playing with the tablets like marbles that wouldn't roll fast enough. A handful clasped, I dared myself. All I'd need was a swallow or two of water to get them down.

I sat frozen, a mocking repeatedly daring me. Assuring me that confusion and pain would finally come to an end.

*If God wanted you, he'd have taken you himself. So, just go on your own.*

A stirring inside grew rough. An anger.

I knew better than that. One must wait for him, his timing. If he didn't take me, then I still must have purpose. And what pain that would cause my family. The thought sickened me. Opening my fist, I let the tablets slip, their pinging ominous. I brushed off the few that stuck to my sweaty palm, the clash scolding my soul.

*These go back to the pharmacy!*

I'd return them as soon as possible.

After an escape up the stairs, my body slumped into a chair in the spare-bedroom-turned-craft-room that had been set up for Sadie. One day, I'd have to clean it up. Not this day. Likely not tomorrow either. Cutouts of fancy paper. Letters and cards, half completed. Her cricket machine still plugged in. Her tumbler of water still waiting for another sip to be taken. Only now, a healthy layer of scuzz lay sleepily atop the liquid.

What was the absorption rate for parents to fully soak in the reality that their child was dead? Surely, I couldn't be the only one resisting. Just how long did it take?

The crank of our metal mailbox at the front door disrupted my emotional crash. Then a car door and its subsequent exit from the driveway. A visitor, perhaps. Had I not heard them knock?

*Get up. Get it together.*

A small box, no bigger than three by five inches, wrapped

with paper and a bow, was wedged inside our mailbox. The metal lid held it steady, given that it didn't fit. A personal delivery. Though an ache still lingered, my lungs were calming from the earlier sobs.

Solace, the next phase of regular outbreaks, wasn't far off. I knew the process well.

I plopped onto the couch, package in my lap, and pulled out the card. A handwritten letter fell to the floor. I wiped my tear-soaked fingers down the sides of my jeans before picking it up. Such artful handwriting across several pages brought a smile. I admired creativity. My penmanship had much to be desired. The letter was from the wife of one of my husband's friends, a lovely woman I, too, considered a friend, even though we didn't know a great deal about each other.

The letter opened with an apology that the delivery had taken so long. She explained her husband kept forgetting to deliver it on his way to the office. She went on to describe their family's trip to South Carolina. As they strolled the beach early on their first day, several people were claiming the remnants of a low tide, mostly beached sand dollars. There had been a storm overnight, so these sea creatures were in plenty. As hard as she tried, she couldn't manage to get one, for the crowd of hunters had already scored them all.

"Then," she wrote, "I coaxed Sadie, in spirit, for assistance. Come on, Sadie, show me a sand dollar."

To her astonishment, one appeared as a wave receded. She was delighted. So much so, she tried it again. A second sand dollar appeared. "I couldn't possibly be so lucky to have a third, but I had to try. And behold, a third!"

But nothing else after that, no fourth to be found. She

cleaned them up, let them dry, and brought them home. A gift for Sadie's mom.

Astonished, I gasped! Thrilled the woman thought of Sadie like that.

*And hey, Sadie, nice work!* My spirits were already lifting.

Inside the small, decorated box, three carefully wrapped items in tissue waited.

My heart raced. Three, in a box!

This was it! This was the gift from Sadie. That morning when she appeared in the upper corner of my bedroom, excitedly jumping up and down, reaching out with a gift box and bow, and counting with her fingers… one, two, three!

My heart raced and fingers shook. A chill traversed my spine. All before a fluid of warmth took its course through my veins. This had to be it! I told no one of that vision—no one.

This was no coincidence. I'd just received a gift from my daughter!

I could barely stand the amazement.

I threw my hands up. "Sadie! Got them!" I called out to the ceiling, my smile unrestrained. "My turn now to be leaping with joy. Thank you, thank you, thank you, honey!"

It was an absolute miracle. These three sand dollars were a gift from my daughter. From Sadie's life in the world beyond that veil, her gift made its way to *me*, and in the shape and form my daughter described. I received this blessing on the absolute worst day of my grief.

What horror—less than an hour ago, I held those tablets in my palm.

*God, thank you. Your timing is so perfect! I went from the lowest of lows to a jubilation of highs!*

The woman who collected them wouldn't have any clue as

to what this gift meant to me. Her husband's so-called forgetfulness granted the absolute optimum timing.

God truly works in mysterious ways. He intercepts our thought life so much more than we're ready to accept. The timing for something we think is delayed could well be the moment he chooses.

Hadn't Jesus said as much to his community in Nazareth in Luke 4—that he'd been sent by God to bind up the brokenhearted? God was serious about lifting us up in better form—and for good reason.

This breeze of life miraculously transformed my day. *God, Jesus, or the Holy Spirit, whichever one of you is responsible, this means so much to me. I don't know how to thank you!*

A full year later, I would discover the traditional storytelling behind a sand dollar. A mysterious tale of faith, a symbol of Jesus Christ's life, death, and resurrection.

The five holes represented the five wounds Christ suffered at crucifixion, each hand, each foot, and the spear in his side. The star pattern symbolized the star of Bethlehem, signaling his birth. The flower image on the sand dollar's opposite side depicted life, his resurrection. One of the myths claimed five fragments resembling doves are on the inside, representing the Holy Spirit.

But I'd never break these open. They'd be protected and pulled out when I needed that lift to remind me of the miraculous. A permanent, earthly reminder, such perfect medicine for a heart of sorrow. A blessed gift.

## 38

READING THROUGH THE Bible wasn't going fast enough. Much to comprehend. Some eye-opening Scriptures. Others, I was well-versed in, and many were head-scratchers. Plugging through the Old Testament, I couldn't help but search for something personal in the messages, to which each fell into one of three categories—a warm edification, a blink fest of befuddlement, or a shocking condemnation.

The local university had a seminary as part of its conglomerate of educational buildings. A few pastors I knew had gone through their programs to prepare themselves for ministerial positions. There, they would be taught a deep understanding of Scripture as well as doctrine, Christian ethics, and church history. In other words, how to interpret the Bible accurately, given the concept and timing of each book written.

I registered for the fall program. Part-time Christian theology. This was my answer, a sure way to boost my absorption of God's Word. Too many ministers, preachers, television evangelists, podcasters, and pamphlets out there with varying messages. Including some wisecrackers. I was after core truths. And nothing but. No longer would I accept anything anyone said and claimed was biblical, no matter how tight or white their collar was. It was time to look at things differently, from God's perspective, if that were even possible. Of course, it wasn't. But I'd attempt just the same.

For a large part, I put aside the line of thinking that I was being punished by God. But surely, he *had* sent me a clear message. It was my pride that he hadn't liked. The fact that I hadn't believed I needed Jesus to get to him.

I wanted nothing more than to study the New Testament and glean more about this special, super being living inside my heart-home. I owed all three at least that much. God for giving his Son, Jesus for moving in, and the Holy Spirit for all his supernatural teachings to make it happen. That was how I saw it.

The course program included the obvious theology studies, but along with the program was church history, family dynamics, and a church admin course. I skipped out of all the latter ones, choosing to attend only the ones focusing on biblical meanings. First, the Old Testament. Then, the New. As if that wasn't enough, I also ordered CD recordings from university professors south of the border who taught religion, specifically Christianity. I continued to watch various religious television programs and documentaries. I admit, I listened and read with a critical and analytical view.

I wasn't trusting what any preacher or professor had to say. Rather, I would dig deep into my research tactics and determine for myself just what I could rely on for a brick of truth. I took most seriously my own experiences. If that was God's Spirit talking to me, then anything I placed in my faith foundation must connect with that *and* align with Scripture.

No sugarcoating.

Vision activity waned practically to nothing. Though my dream activity picked up considerably. I chuckled, wondering if that was God's way to wean me off his directness now that I was focusing on his Word and employing my will.

Visions were more forceful, having bluntness and clarity, their messages carrying a lasting emotional weight. Dreams, on the other hand, had varying intensities, were less direct, and often felt like a puzzle intended for solving. Plus, they could disintegrate almost immediately. Those ones, should they lack an image for contemplation, I discarded.

I was trying desperately to get back to a life, to establish a new and supportive family normal. We had all been mourning. My brain literally hurt—I swore half the cells up there in that head of mine had died. Evening courses, papers, and exams, on top of getting back to a taxing full-time job, demanded a great deal. I still cried a lot, mostly during the commute to and from work, often playing the song "Somewhere over the Rainbow" to make things sting a little more.

Guilt sometimes had its way of washing me with selfish desire. I much preferred to have taken care of my daughter forever than to have her gone from my embrace. Mind you, notwithstanding those debilitating spasms! Still, I wasn't "relieved" when Sadie passed, as several well-wishing coworkers suggested had to be the case.

Despite everything God had done for me, all the divine messages and happenstances, I still found myself imprisoned in that deep black pit the storm had spat me into. The surrounding walls, a familiar bleakness, the ground a viscous layer of wet muck. I was getting far too comfortable in there. I'd read many articles stating parents never get over the death of their child. The thought of this place being my forever home was daunting. I was desperate to build a new one.

One weekend morning, I awoke with a different song playing in my head. I relished the familiar tune, one Sadie loved—Sarah McLachlan's "Ordinary Miracle." Sadie listened to it a thousand times along with Bon Jovi's "Living on a Prayer," her other fav. One particular phrase in the tune got louder, more distinct than the others, as though to instruct: "Write down your dreams…"

Huh?

I hadn't recalled this phrase when hearing that song countless times before. Needing to confirm my suspicion, I found the song on YouTube. As I suspected, the words in my dream were not the musician's words at all. The actual phrase was close, however, as it told us not to throw away our dreams, but rather to hold them close in our hearts.

A pretty clever way for God to instruct me to journal all dreams.

I placed a request. "When it does come time for me to abide with you, might you consider me for a job? One where I could work on that team of yours to decide the hows and ways to cleverly deliver your messages!"

Now, *that* would be super fun.

So, rather than closing off my journaling, given visions had slowed considerably, I picked it back up. Writing dreams was so much harder. Visions remained clear, while dreams vanished. Mornings were now spent on scrambling with paper and pen to capture as many details as possible, noting items that stood out, and even colors that stole the show.

I was glad I did. My reward, an abundance of learning came from several dreams—

I was back at that nasal cave! The large boulder still aside the opening. Though the interior appeared dark, I knew if I walked inside, I'd soon be blinded by the light of a beautiful world, heaven, God's home. Or at least the sure path to get there. Jesus wasn't waiting this time, but a hand directed me to walk *around* the cave in a specific direction, opposite clockwise. I watched myself do so. When I came around the other side, I was holding an open Bible, reading as I walked. My mouth wide, speaking aloud the words. It appeared I was representing a pastor or preacher of some sort.

"Oh no," I heard myself say. "Father, you've got the wrong girl!"

I laughed. Not at him, of course, but at me. I couldn't see myself in that type of role, a ministering one. He must be mistaken. This was something I couldn't do.

Then I realized the overzealous interpretation. It was more of a seeking, studying walk I was taking.

Okay, I could handle that. In fact, I'd already started.

The opposing direction to clockwise disturbed me, particularly when God had asked me once to turn around and directed the clockwise position. I'd tuck this directional note away. Surely, something would eventually make sense of it. Perhaps it was more of an east or west thing, the concept of a clockface likely not in existence for purposes of Scripture.

Though I imagined God was up-to-date with all of the world's progress.

Another dream I experienced could have come from a sci-fi movie, a genre I rarely watched—

A couple of somebodies were standing behind me. They picked me up, out of my body. Next thing I knew, I was inside a bustling arena full of humanlike beings of every size, some with wings, many without. Each on a mission of some sort, a task in mind. Like a celestial ensemble, they moved and churned in perfect harmony, no one bumping into the other. I presumed to be somewhere in heaven.

And then I spotted her. Sadie at a young age, like when she was eight.

Two strange beings walked past, and their eagle-like heads and hunched backs interrupted my view. Something was wrapped around their shallow foreheads, like receivers. Lean and thin, though anything but scrawny, they both appeared incredibly powerful and reminded me of ambulance drivers. Their job now done, they'd delivered their patient, whom I believed was me.

The crowd of bodies paid me little attention, and I searched to catch another glimpse. Yes, it was Sadie! I was delighted to see her face. Her hair short and brown, not quite as I'd known her hair at that age, but the same height. I thought anyway. Her eyes were on fire—a glazing blue. Considerably bluer than the hazel green when she was alive with me.

She beelined through the crowd to me. Her arms caught my waist, and when she hugged me so tight, I hugged her back. This time I wasn't letting go. She missed me. I felt that in her hug, saw it in her expression. I told her not to worry, everything would be fine. She was part of "them" now, all of them in fully white garments. I didn't let go. Rather, the dream vanished as I hung on.

It was odd, felt like a role reversal. Me, the earthling, telling her, the one in heaven not to worry, all was good, all would be fine. And in the dream, I meant it. Like another part of me was speaking.

I acknowledged some key things: That within my soul all was well and as it was planned to be. I embraced the enlightenment. These dreams were revealing things about me, that innermost persona, as well as general lessons and tidbits of a grander picture. That we all have a place, a purpose, a role.

Then again, might that dream have simply reflected my regret for our last hug, that I hadn't hugged her as long and tight as I would've if I'd known it were our last? Some psychological want. To be transported to heaven to have a second chance for our last hug?

I considered the next dream to be more of the cautionary sort—

In some kind of wall-less manufacturing environment, wheat was being collected and ground into cups spaced evenly along a conveyor belt. Someone, several workers actually, was placing mice into a large chopper and using the ground-up results as a sealer to pour atop the cups of grain. It was a deceitful method of topping the good with evil. The whole process was incredibly well-organized and efficient. Many were accepting these cups, a form of bread, spiritual food for life. The recipients, unaware of the seal's ingredients, considered these disgusting sealed cups of wheat socially acceptable.

A definite message of caution for the trickery of deceit when it came to one's spiritual diet.

Around the same time, I experienced several dreams leaving me with an end-times feel. I would escape disasters of fire and ash but only at the last moment, rather, the last millisecond, to be more precise. The dread of a coming judgment pushed with greater urgency for insight and a craving for wisdom.

One particular dream changed my thinking as to how my soul, that old and poor woman, fit into this scheme of existence—

Skateboarding, of all things, was what I was doing, grooving happily along a grassy nook. Tells you how much I know about skateboarding. Pretty sure one cannot do such on grass. Perhaps it was more of a hoverboard, only inches above the ground. Whatever. Suddenly, the crest of a hill appeared, and I had zero brakes!

I was *not* calm; I was panicking.

On a decline and picking up speed, I zipped along toward a cliff to nowhere.

It was inevitable. I was about to go airborne, and only God knew what would happen.

You'd think I would've awakened just before disaster struck. But no. Across the threshold, I went. Flew into midair.

Then nothing but dead silence.

Strangely, like a spark in water, my fear was abruptly snuffed out.

Curiosity peaked, a demonstration began, and it was no longer personal. I witnessed the symbolic whole of a being separate into three components, each taking a different direction.

Down went the skateboard. No bottom to the chasm, at least none to my vision. Surely, it smashed into bits at some point, sank into deep waters, or disintegrated. It didn't seem to matter. There was no need for it any further.

A delicate orb, whimsical and translucent, like a bubble released from a child's soapy wand, floated upward and meandered aloft. Ecstatic to be free at long last. A living wingless entity with graceful energy. It took a curious look at me, and I sensed its mind saying, "See! I exist."

The third and most familiar-feeling component just hung there. My attention shifted to it, and my concern ratcheted up just watching it struggle. Also, translucent and orb-like, only larger, it hung, dazed and with the weight of want, too heavy to float upward. Also looking my way and, I sensed, wondering why it wasn't able.

Would the little orb allow that larger one to hitch on to its energy flow?

It didn't appear so; it was as if they'd just been sliced apart.

## 39

Hours floated by as they might for an artist releasing from his mind a captive rendering to an awaiting canvas. Only no canvas was spacious enough for the imagination conjuring inside my head.

The skateboard dream came with a filling of inspired thoughts, provoking ideas thick with imagery. A new path to forage, about to take on a life of its own.

What happened at death? Hadn't I craved to know? Wouldn't any mother who was blocked from witnessing their child's safety beyond the veil?

Perhaps this was it, the instant of separation, when one left their body at the moment of death. Physical death. Earthly death. *The* great separation.

I walked through possible scenarios, considering where and if alignment with Scripture existed.

First, there was the simple bit, the skateboard.

Surely it symbolized the body, the vehicle to carry one's soul. Flesh and bones with the veins and all the other whatnots. Simply that of which is temporary and goes back to dust. After all, Adam, the first man God made, was formed from the earth. Down the skateboard went off that cliff. "And the dust returns to the ground it came from," (Ecclesiastes 12:7a). Though a Mack truck might have been a more secure way to travel through life. And not that one's body doesn't matter. It does. A great deal. It just didn't in this dream. And given my witness to the horror cancer does to a body, I didn't mind that this particular component was subjected to the rule of gravity.

I put the vehicle piece aside. There was much more to consider. Most notably, its unprotected state, a skateboard no less. No wonder we are so vulnerable to physical harm.

I sank into a sunroom chair and leaned into the quiet stillness.

What if the larger of the two orb-like spheres was a soul, and the small one, the accompanying spirit? After all, a breath from God provided the spark to which Adam came to life.

God's breath, a spirit.

Adam's life, a soul.

Two invisible components mystically intertwined and embedded inside one visible body.

A working theory.

"Then the Lord God formed a man from the dust of the ground and breathed into his nostrils the breath of life, and the man became a living being" (Genesis 2:7). Three components to make a human being. Countless theologians and the Scriptures seem to agree. Spirit, soul, and body, the three primary ingredients that make up a human being. Nothing earth-shattering and already widely accepted.

Scripture confirmed it. We were made up of three components. "May your whole spirit, soul and body be kept blameless at the coming of our Lord Jesus Christ" (1 Thessalonians 5:23b).

So this must be the pinnacle of my dream, the coming apart at physical death.

The way those two orbs were alive, vivid with separate personalities, said much. The small one came with a deeper level of thinking, plus a higher standard when it came to morals. More divine. And *impatient*. It didn't appear too interested in waiting around. Rather, it simply wanted to escape quickly and get back to where it came from. It belonged to God. That small one was no doubt the spirit.

Hmm, I pictured it reentering that cave, the nostril of God. "And the spirit returns to God who gave it" (Ecclesiastes 12:7b).

Though that little guy was sarcastic. I did catch its snicker, a duh-get-it-now? look toward its larger counterpart.

The large orb just hung there, bobbing up and down as though it were navigating survival on the surface of deep waters, knowing it couldn't float forever and looking around for answers. Notably at me.

My turn for a "Duh, like I should know." Was there a life jacket somewhere?

This strange scenario wasn't anything I'd given much thought to before. But there they were, two orbs—for lack of a better label—unattached and distinctly individual. Each with their own persona, their own story to tell, and since they'd been separated, their own destination.

It seemed likely, however, that remaining blameless didn't mean coming apart. The two had been intricately joined when riding along on its skateboard, but now, separated. The spirit had the capability to float up to the heavens; the soul did not. The latter had lost its hitch, abandoned in midair. It simply hadn't the capability to float upward on its own. Far too heavy with the weight of the world inside it.

The spirit, God's breath, always returned to the same destination from where it came.

The soul, man's persona, could go either way. Carried up to the heavens with its partnered-up spirit or fall to the dust with its beloved skateboard. Hmm, two interesting options, an age-old debate.

I blew out an exhale. Only God could slice the two apart. And it was obvious—the goal was to stay connected with the spirit God has given. Made sense to build up the spirit and find ways to lighten the weight of the soul, so to speak. Symbolically, anyway.

Jesus assured the thief on the cross aside him, his soul would carry to heaven. "Truly I tell you, today you will be with me in paradise" (Luke 23:43). This was after the criminal, who admitted his own punishment, challenged why Christ was being punished for doing no wrong. He further asked Jesus to remember him once he arrived in his kingdom.

Believing is key. Critical to ensuring one's soul can be carried up and be present with Jesus. If not, perhaps those who fall are the ones who sleep in the dust. "And many of those who sleep in the dust of the earth shall awake, some to everlasting life, and some to shame and everlasting contempt" (Daniel 12:2). Perhaps God was claiming to deal with them later.

Was it that elementary? How did one ensure their soul remained securely attached to their spirit? In fact, how did one even know their spirit?

Outright uncanny. I couldn't help but laugh. The concept of taking personal revelations from dreams and tying them to Scripture, so simple symbolisms could lurk in the mind's forefront. Such handy reminders filled with the essence of truth, the kind that edified and pointed the way. A kind of knowledge that bypassed logic.

But hey, one must be ready for the day of their own great separation! I recalled two instances in Sadie's final days when she claimed someone was holding her right hand.

"No, Mama, don't sit there," she'd said once as I took the seat aside her recliner. She grinned. "Someone's sitting there and they're holding my hand." While no one was there visibly or physically, she said the sensation of her hand clasped the way it was gave her a strong sense of peace and calm and made her feel safe.

The second time was in the car, traveling with her dad. "I felt someone holding my hand the whole way," she confessed. Someone in the invisible world was there with her, holding her. Letting her know she would never be alone. "But I was worried since there was no room in the passenger seat. I hoped they weren't having to run or fly outside while we were driving!"

I just shook my head. "Oh, Sadie."

Incredibly thankful I was, knowing Sadie's soul had been lifted, she was alive in paradise with Jesus. And with special privileges, it seemed. Likely due to that persistent persona of her soul.

Plus, good to know too, it was the second death, the death of one's soul that one truly needed to be concerned with. "Do not fear those who kill the body but cannot kill the soul. Rather fear him who can destroy both body and soul in hell" (Matthew 10:28).

Obviously, more was to come with this mindful illustration. God wasn't done yet.

## 40

Sure, this was a risk.

At the kitchen sink, the water a little too hot, I balled the washcloth into a coffee cup, slipping from too much soap. There they were—those three little yellow finches on my deck post again! Oh my, how special to see them this morning. Were they building their nests, like I was building my heart-home?

Who built their house of faith from dreams and visions? Images connected to Scriptures and what? Inner notions of what was true and what was not? It was the best I could go on, particularly as my past building methods failed me.

It was time to take God's messages to the next level. Stop waving them away when convenient. The stakes were real. Sadie did say to me, "Just wait, Mama. It'll come."

*I'm counting on it, honey.*

"Ouch!" The fragile cup broke, cutting into a knuckle. I wrapped it with a drying cloth, and instead of reaching for bandages, I took a seat in that place of refuge, my sunroom. That analytical side of my mind was not about to give up simply because of a little blood.

Reviewing God's Word from a historical and fact-based point of view was helpful. As was continuing my introspective read-through of the Holy Bible.

I closed my eyes and leaned back, stuffing an extra cushion behind me for support. The spirit component, that little orb, was particularly intriguing. I couldn't let go of that image and my belief that it wanted me to know more. God's own breath. Invisible, likely even to one's soul, yet it had such critical purposes. God's eyes on us.

"Through this connection, he knows everything that comes into our minds," I whispered aloud, though no one was home to hear anyway.

I chuckled. "That spirit within us is a personal reporter. Every thought and word that ended up written in that book he has on each one of us."

I imagined an old-fashioned reporter with a pencil skirt. What was the name of that lady in the *Superman* comics? Both feisty and charming.

"For who knows a person's thoughts except their own spirit within them?" (1 Corinthians 2:11a). That book with gold-rimmed pages enshrined atop a pedestal was where I imaged thoughts were uploaded to, where that scribe recorded it all.

I stood. My drying towel was soaked in bright red. I definitely need that bandage. As I climbed the stairs, I was reminded that effective highways of communication run both ways. Wouldn't that spirit of ours also be our receiver? Perfect for information downloads—the pass into our soul for God-breathed dreams and visions. "But it is the spirit in a person, the breath of the Almighty, that gives them understanding" (Job 32:8).

Hey, it fit.

As I sat on the edge of a bathtub, tending to my wounded knuckle, I laughed at myself. Trying to sort out the truths of the universe. Though, it must be part of his thing. God invited the pursuit of divine truths and, to do so, encouraged the use of the ears and eyes of one's own spirit.

Physiologically, who can say how this works? Like opening

a window to another realm so sight and sound could enter with the wind.

With a wrapped knuckle, I decided folding laundry was a better option than finishing the dishes right now.

That spirit within us was the link between our soul and God. And… it *tells* on us. Reports back everything. As children, we often hear "no tattling." Either this was a skipped lesson for spirits in spirit school, or God's ways were simply not ours.

I smirked. It was the latter, obviously. Our spirits like to tattle.

The contents from the dryer smelled fresh as I clutched them to my chest before dumping it all onto my bed.

Nothing our persona thinks or battles with is hidden, nor is anything our body does or any mutterings our tongue might spatter, nor even what our eyes see. All is transferred knowledge straight up to the heavens. For a little translucent bubble, that spirit gifted at birth had a pretty big job.

I shoved a pile of folded bath towels into the linen closet, then plopped into a seated position atop my mattress. My mind was adamant not to let this line of thinking disintegrate.

Considering the image burned in my mind, that spirit was incapable of lifting the soul upward even if it wanted to. Clearly, it wasn't allowed. There had to be something the Scriptures said about this.

Hours went by as I flipped through Bible pages. The phone rang at least five times. I let the answering machine capture the callers' wants. Far too immersed to be disturbed or pushed off track, I was too shocked with one particular finding: the spirit one receives at birth is considered *dead*.

A bit creepy, indeed.

A soul carrying around a dead spirit does not sound overly enlightening.

This was how we began at birth?

Widespread understanding that I'd grown up with, perhaps just assumed, included God's spark being alive within us at birth, be it however magical or mysterious. I was finding it difficult to pinpoint any Scripture verses to confirm this. Hesitantly, I tossed that belief. It had been smashed to bits anyhow with my house and was one of those broken pieces splayed at my feet.

So, it seems he was naturally part of us, given the spirit came from him, and though that spirit performed its function, it was considered defunct. Empty. Not alive. Dead. It might have come from him and worked for him, but was now separated from him. And separation from God equals *dead*.

Even dead spirits are returned to God at the time of one's death. Alive or dead, all spirits belong to him. He makes that clear.

Needing a stretch, I jostled up and down the stairs a couple times. Heart pounding, I got back at it.

"Okay, so..." I took a settling breath. "We are born with a soul and a dead spirit inside our bodies." I announced my great and unusual discovery to the empty house and then continued in thought. "God has a dear want for us—to receive a new spirit to wake up the one we were given at birth, one that will allow it to accept all that God has to offer us."

By now, it was late in the afternoon. I'd let the entire day be spent with mental meanderings. Yet I felt richer for it. Still, I needed to get those dishes done. There sat that broken cup, the one that caused me to bleed.

I likened one's spirit to an empty cup, in many cases, a

shattered one. One's cup must become whole and ready to hold the pourings of God's Spirit.

Perhaps this was where free will is offered to the soul of every human. The choice given—where to go to fill that cup.

## 41

Finally, I began to attend church again. It happened to be a baptism day. As the pastor carried the baby up and down the aisle for us all to admire, I had to wonder, what benefit did that ceremony truly provide?

I escaped just as the sermon ended, from the back pew out the back door. The threat of tears would loom otherwise. Sadie had sat on the council representing the youth a few years back. I recall her rant, "We need music for our generation, stuff we can relate to." Our church had prayed for her consistently over the time of her ill-health, and for that, I was ever grateful. So much generosity and kindness they gifted us. But that didn't mean I was ready to face them all over post-service coffee and cake. Not just yet.

The pastor's reading left me with one resonating verse. "Jesus answered, 'Very truly I tell you, no one can enter the kingdom of God unless they are born of water and the Spirit. Flesh gives birth to flesh, but the Spirit gives birth to spirit'" (John 3:5–6).

Two baptisms? Had Sadie gone through both, not symbolically, but spiritually? What were God's stipulations?

The odds were said to be anywhere in the one-to-a-million range by the time a sperm and an egg did their thing, to create a human delivered through the waters of pregnancy. Every single person was nothing short of an incredible statistical miracle. If only everyone could let that soak in. Was this the "born of water" Jesus spoke of? One enters the world this way to gain life, as said "with painful labor you will give birth to children" (Genesis 3:16b).

Hmm, fits and at the same time, it doesn't.

A car honked and came to a screeching halt. Apparently, I cut him off as I pulled out of the church driveway. So much for my quiet exit. *Focus, Hanna, focus!*

Sometimes it's much easier *not* to consider some of this stuff.

My husband and I chatted over a second coffee once I got home. "I've heard that, when someone felt an empty void, despite having everything they've ever wanted—a loving relationship, a generous load of friends, and even a fulfilling career—all can appear as well as well can be on the outside. But inside, a lack of meaning exists, a depression, a disconnect from whatever was supposed to matter."

He concurred and reminded me of someone we both knew who fit that scenario.

Perhaps that's the achiness of an empty cup craving to be filled.

There was no denying the theme existed within the Scriptures that one's empty cup must be dealt with. A natural human inclination.

Needing to attend an errand, my husband stepped out for an hour. Enough time for me to soak myself in the sunroom, allow my heart and head space to debate.

I picked up my sketch pad and pen from the end table. Could I draw the formulation in my head? Oh, the drawback of being a visual thinker, slow to process lest an image could provide the big picture perspective. *Course, God, you made me this way!*

A two-stepper.

First, a fillable cup, a prepared vessel renewed by Christ. I jostled a chuckle, reminding myself of Jesus fixing the hole beneath my shag carpet in my heart-home.

Then second, the actual filling. In no time, a recollection surfaced. The socially accepted and widely manufactured form of deceit from that dream weeks ago stirred up an uneasiness. Wheat collected into cups and sealed with ground-up rodents. Were most people accepting this form of filling, and worse, had I, too, been tricked in the past?

My knees felt the chill first. I wrapped my arms around myself. More desperate than ever for simple, God-inspired visuals to rely on, a safe place to exist.

Even Indiana Jones chose wisely in the legendary movie involving the search for a mystical Holy Grail. "That's the cup of a carpenter," the simple wooden cup said to be that from which Jesus drank in the story of the Last Supper. Hollywood aside, Christ made it clear that a rebirthing of one's spirit is required to make it suitable for the filling of God's own spirit.

Perhaps this was representative of the two forms of baptism? The cup and the pour. Christ and the Holy Spirit.

*Makes sense, but stop it, Hanna. Go make a late lunch.*

Hmm... Egg salad or ham sandwiches?

My skirt caught on the edge of a bottle in the built-in wine rack as I hurried past the kitchen island. Hmm, there was the wedding story where the host ran out of wine before the evening was over. Jesus instructed the purification jars be filled then he turned the water to wine.

A wonderful vintage I'd imagine.

A Cabernet, perhaps.

He'd noted this act was before his time, most likely as it

preceded the coming of the Holy Spirit who would take his place for the actual pour.

Placing six eggs into a pot of water, I couldn't help but feel thankful.

Sadie loved Jesus. She invited the Holy Spirit to enter. I was witness to it. Thank heavens. My lips curved up as I turned the burner to high.

I stood in front of the stove, reflecting on this transformation, then rushed back to the sunroom, picked up that pen and sketched a column, simple as a child's drawing.

At the bottom, a skateboard—the body of flesh, returning to dust.

Above it, a circle with ribbon—a gifted soul.

Then, a cracked cup with a frown—the spirit received at birth, broken and separated from God.

Christ enters, the Carpenter, repairing the holes. Happy face smile on a whole cup. A stroke of disregard for the old cup.

From above, a bottle pours—the Spirit filling the cup with blessings and wisdom.

And at the top, God's hand stretched down, holding it all together.

A lifeline from heaven to earth.

I laughed at my drawing, though I appreciated what the column represented. A tall posture for one to keep in place. The new cup ready for the pouring in of God's Spirit, the utmost crucial links. The two baptisms, the cup and the pour. Christ and the Spirit. One requires both.

Oops, the eggs were boiling over. I scurried back to the kitchen and turned off the stove. Draining the hot water from the pot, I added a handful of ice cubes, a trick I'd learned to make peeling eggs easy. I buttered four pieces of bread, my mind trying desperately to put this business to bed. But all I could think of was that chained link of power. A welcomed illumination. A lifeline, not just coming straight from God himself, but to him as well. Surely with that in place, there'd be no problem for that little spirit orb to carry up that large soul orb, no matter how weighty. "But we have this treasure in jars of clay to show that this all-surpassing power is from God and not from us" (2 Corinthians 4:7).

I could picture now how one didn't have to be *good* enough in God's eyes. Instead, one required all the parties to be accounted for and in attendance in that vertical pillar of faith.

Smashing the eggs with onion and mayo, I wondered still: Who could even know their own spirit? Anyone ever caught a glimpse? It seemed a challenge enough to have the desire to glimpse one's own soul for fear of what they'd see, much less give thought to the characteristics and appearance of one's spirit.

Especially if it's dead. Well, broken and parched. Severed from God.

I mixed in a squeeze of mustard and splattered the concoction onto the waiting bread slices.

If only we could see those parts of ourselves in the mirror. But our true identity is hidden from even ourselves according to the Scriptures. "For now we see only a reflection as in a mirror; then we shall see face to face. Now I know in part; then I shall know fully, even as I am fully known" (1 Corinthians 13:12).

The garage door opened. Perfect timing. Hubby was home, and sandwiches were ready. At least our stomachs will get filled.

## 42

Sadie had wept from a hinting that sin was the root of her illness.

All along, I'd misunderstood sin, believing it was one of those traditional religious mysterious things that had a good dose of supporting biblical research by many scholars.

*Whatever—or rather, however.*

Sin was said to transfer into bodily afflictions. All more suitably reserved for the likes of those who abused, murdered, stole from their neighbors, or perhaps even those who swore excessively in God's name. Though a strong theme within the Scriptures claimed that no one could be sinless. It was an impossibility. We lived in a world made of a chaotic mixture, good and evil. We did not come inherent with a sifter of sorts.

How did Adam start this ball rolling? More symbolism for the state of the world. He ate from the Tree of Knowledge of Good and Evil. He fed off this mixture of good and evil.

One key basic rule of God's: nothing with evil mixed within could get close to him. Not only did that mean Adam, given his diet, it included any soul. Even today.

Perhaps that's why God said right at the get-go to Adam, "You shall surely die." The man's soul had no hope of rising. An event later dubbed as the Fall of Man. Jesus wasn't around yet to replace anyone's broken cup, nor the Holy Spirit to pour into it. Early days.

It must have saddened God to kick Adam out of his garden. But you can understand why danger lurked. If he didn't block Adam from also digesting fruit from the Tree of Life—everlasting life—the future of eternity would suffer indeed.

Imagine eternity filled with evil still lurking, a never-ending chaotic mix. No thank you.

I laughed at my elementary ideology. Surely, I'd fail this theology course.

It seemed to me that God's entire goal was to build a family who loved him, a heavenly household of sons and daughters. A home with zero evil lurking about. Hence, his dilemma, how to follow his own rules and allow those willing and wanting a way back into his garden, a way for their soul orbs to rise.

Yes, this was a grave matter. That evil snake was a pressing contender, wanting the same thing. Only his leadership was without God or Jesus or the Spirit of truth. Rather, cleverly, the snake himself was deceitful and eager to be the leader of the world.

Though lectures at the seminary took on differing theories, my mind absorbed only what fit into the spiritual illustration I was creating, my own house of faith, flash images for daily reminders as to what was important. If there was logic that fit in nicely with Scripture and those illuminating dreams and visions, I snatched it up.

As to my personal findings and explanations, I kept most of them to myself for fear of being laughed at. *"Just a grieving mother making Scripture work to her liking,"* they might say. *"Her need, simply to find a purpose in her child's death."*

But to me, it was far more.

Continuing with studies on themes of sin in the Scripture,

I found three in particular to be arresting, each causing me a hard swallow.

Number 1: Worrying. It sounds so illogical, but we all do it—carrying that extra weight in our souls over something that hasn't happened yet.

The Holy Spirit has gone to the trouble of marking a soul as God's, a win for the team. A mighty feat.

Then that soul goes about displaying signs of anxiousness and hopelessness. I'm guessing it doesn't go over well. The more I read about this spirit of God's, the more it was obvious he had a persona of his own, one we could disappoint, frustrate, and even sadden. Once he made that guarantee to lift a soul orb to heaven, the least one could do in return was avoid adding more to its heaviness. "And do not grieve the Holy Spirit of God, by whom you were sealed for the day of redemption" (Ephesians 4:30). "Do not be anxious about anything, but in every situation, by prayer and petition, with thanksgiving, present your requests to God" (Philippians 4:6).

A wrestling indeed, certainly for mothers everywhere. Perhaps it's just psychological conditioning. After all, mothers are known to be branded worriers.

Number 2: Grief. Yikes! While grief wasn't a sin, thematic was the command for grief. Deep groaning sorrow was to be of a temporary nature. Jesus was adamant that we do not forget what's been promised to those who believe, that they've passed into the presence of God. Ignoring this was another form of neglect, not to be confused with a keeping-up-appearances attitude. And so, at every funeral service, sometimes there'd be an elephant in the room—did that person who died believe? Thank heavens the Scriptures were clear: even the tiniest seed of belief could be powerful.

I vowed not to be a parent who grieved their child daily for the rest of their days on earth. Nothing good could come of that. An early death or some kind of terminal illness, as research suggests, can strike grieving parents but would only stir up even more grief for the family. I'd eventually get out of this pit, and the joy I prayed for would indeed arrive.

Number 3: Love. Perhaps not a sin per se, though a prescription for uprightness. We were commanded to love God above all others. Not that many months ago, as if a mountain too steep to scale, that was one tall order. To place those three—God, Holy Spirit, Jesus—at the top of my love chart, above my husband, children, parents, friends, and yes, even above the child taken?

More wrestling for sure.

Though none other could do what these three had done for me, none other could provide comfort and peace, nor wisdom as these. And none other could offer a loving, eternal home. "Anyone who loves their father or mother more than me is not worthy of me; anyone who loves their son or daughter more than me is not worthy of me" (Matthew 10:37).

As if inner sparring with oneself wasn't enough, one must also keep watchful for even those in their own household! Jesus warned a few times about what conflict to expect. "A man's enemies are the members of his own household" (Micah 7:6b). "Do you think that I have come to give peace on earth? No, I tell you, but rather division. For from now on in one house there will be five divided, three against two and two against three" (Luke 12:51–52).

Was this symbolic, a parable for one's own faith house? Were the two against three, representative of a soul and its human spirit wrestling with those critical others, the divine three wanting to win the battle? Or as Jesus continues to explain, one's own earthly family. Either way, he gives a dire warning to guard one's soul. Isn't it through family that we take on worries, anxieties, ideologies, even fears? Hadn't Adam done that with Eve?

I was discovering it was far easier to hold a simple belief in Jesus than to absorb all of his Word. And I'd barely scratched the surface. However, although steep, his Word and commands represented ladder rungs, a way out of this chasm where tall walls of slippery, wet mud surrounded me.

Keep at it, I encouraged myself. I needed to climb out of this pit. And—*stay* out!

# 43

Over the next four months, I began to call him Adonai.

He was my father now, and I, his daughter. As I wanted something more personal, it felt right. Of course, there were other Old Testament names, ways God had been addressed—Elohim, Yahweh, El Shaddai. But I'm more at home with Adonai. As for Jesus, I began to call him Lord. An odd social stigma bothered me. Sadly, the name of Jesus came with awkward branding. Perhaps I'd heard it in vain over the years far too many times. He deserved greater respect, and until my mind could free itself from "old things," I reverenced him as Lord.

Time slugged. An old turtle carrying a shell heavier than it was built for, but at least it was moving. No longer did it feel so fresh, as though Sadie died early yesterday morning. Now, it felt as if it had happened perhaps nearly a week ago, though it had been several months.

I was drawing upon that seed of peace promised by Jesus, another thematic commitment from the Bible, hoping that one day it'd grow into a tree I could relax beneath and neither time nor season would matter for any reason. Though my inner sense begged otherwise. *Don't get comfy down here. This pit is not the place to grow seeds of any kind, much less build a home.*

My wrestling kept me coming back to Romans 8:18: "I consider that our present sufferings are not worth comparing with the glory that will be revealed in us."

I supposed I should be thankful for any suffering that came my way, sometimes even letting my mind go back to much earlier years. Childhood angst—those bad seeds of anger and unforgiveness, of shame and worthlessness—I'd pushed way down, deep. Thinking it couldn't grow in the dark. The fog lifting from Sadie's passing exposed those unhealthy roots. The seeds had grown. Burying them hadn't suffocated their want. Now I sat in the dark along with them while they fed off my weakness, eager to bind me. Those invisible enemies finally had me where they wanted.

Struck down I might be, but not destroyed.

Still so many questions. If the measurement degree of suffering was equivalent to the degree of blessing on a pendulum swing, then I might do okay when it came to heavenly rewards. *Ha! At least I still have a sense of humor, can still look at the bright side.*

From God's perspective, I bet Jesus's crucifixion was the outermost boundary on the suffering side of a pendulum's sway, while sitting on the right-hand side of God was the boundary for the highest reward, the greatest blessing. That which was given to Christ. As for humanity, the rest of us can likely place our swing degree of suffering and rewards somewhere inside that pendulum sway. Whether suffering must occur to gain rewards, well, that's a debate for the theologians. Good thing though, "The Lord is close to the broken hearted" (Psalm 34:18a), and that, in itself, was a blessing I experienced firsthand, proven to be true.

It would be interesting to understand, even symbolically, how God measured our suffering, our rewards, or any part of us, for that matter. The more I read, the more I was convinced God was just as concerned with *how* one handled and responded, maybe more so than *what* happened to them. Not that he didn't care. He did. Regardless, he expected responsibility. To love, to give, to care, to forgive, plus several other things.

But forgiveness was indeed a biggie. I was sure of that. To shed the weight of a darkened soul.

Daniel, a faithful man in the Bible known for receiving powerful visions from God, once interpreted the mysterious handwriting on a wall, a message for a king who praised false gods. *MENE, MENE, TEKEL, PARSIN* announced in public the results of a divine scale. "You have been weighed on the scales and found wanting" (Daniel 5:27).

I bet his soul orb was heavy.

Then there's the famous measuring line and plumb line that God referenced to the prophet Isaiah. "I will make justice the measuring line and righteousness the plumb line" (Isaiah 28:17a).

The plumb line, a carpenter's tool to measure perfect vertical alignment. Easy one. I'd add in the alignment requirement to that envisioned pillar I'd sketched, flesh at the bottom, the almighty Creator at the top. That body, soul, Jesus-awakened-spirit, a pour-of-living-truth, and an intimate-tie-to-God-himself link. I wasn't creating a human tower, but rather an illustration for spiritual reminders, for those moments when my soul felt burdened and heavy. A way to review Scripture and let it fall into place. Jesus spoke in parables, and after all, pictures could say far more than words ever could.

I was pleased once I came across a verse in Proverbs, affirming my personal illustration. "The name of the Lord is a fortified tower; the righteous run to it and are safe" (Proverbs 18:10).

Justice, the measuring line, would take more thought. Though a good point to incorporate are the words of Jesus, cautioning all that how one measured others with judgment would be the measuring tool used on themselves. "For in the same way you judge others, you will be judged, and with the measure you use, it will be measured to you" (Matthew 7:2).

*Yikes! So, no judging. Ever. Warning duly noted.*

Just why the surfacing of that Jake character came about, provoking my thoughts, jabbed as though wanting to break down my defenses. He came to me from his grave, generations past, to request forgiveness. That ghostly visit, his begging reach, the mysterious ancestral link, well, it all poked holes in my theories, challenging the new foundation I was constructing. Something was unsettling about the whole thing. Might his soul have fallen with his physical body at his time of separation, and now he was working on lightening it up?

But that didn't resonate with anything biblical. Unless, of course, the biblical meaning of "sleeping in the dust" was symbolic of "wandering the earth" as ghosts—lost souls—are amply reported to be doing.

Another query worthy of a good shrug.

Perhaps my continued review of Scriptures and theology studies would spring a fitting enlightenment. Right now, Jake and his begging just didn't fit into any logic. Nor did those invisible hatchet attacks from long ago.

## 44

We'd reached the year-one anniversary, and that ever-watching beast of grief continued to hang around.

Like a leopard on the hunt, its usual trick was to lie low, wait for the perfect moment, then ambush with quick bursts. Muscular paws prolonged the attack as if it were all a game to beat its own clocked record—how long could it drag out its play to gnaw away its victim's will for life this time? One minute, five, perhaps fifteen?

People told me time would be a healer. I found it quite the opposite. Time became a new sort of enemy, though this one didn't hide, then attack. No, time was gutsier. Unlike the solitary beast who hid and lurched from darkness, time settled itself out in the open and got everyone and everything onside with its cruel taunts. How unfair for minutes and hours, days and months, to carry on as though nothing happened. The anniversary was approaching, and tension was building. I'd made so much progress and was afraid of hurtling back to the starting block.

Of course, then I looked around.

*I'm still here. Yesterday's gone. Don't want tomorrow, a dank fog still clinging to my skin. Have I made progress?*

The sunroom was still my favorite place to sit. The house quiet and hollow, I closed my eyes. Wasn't it just yesterday when Sadie asked for that cup of orange juice? When she laughed with a friend on the phone? When she yelled "bucket" and got me scrambling to catch the result of her nausea?

With some kind of misplaced honor, I pulled out my journal and recounted all the events of Sadie's passing, the days before, the day of, the days after. All raw and numbing triggers. I might've been smarter to review the large stack of lovely cards and notes. Indeed, that would have been much kinder to myself, far more comforting.

I came across a vision clip, one of those profound snapshots. I read the journal entry—

Words appeared in front of me, large letterings in an open book. The black ink on parchment disintegrated, one partial line lingered just enough to catch it, "…with all the madness in our world, still nothing beats the hollowness that intertwines with death."

Quite poetic, whoever wrote it. It was nothing I'd read before.

With the planted reminder to caution the heaviness of grief, I pulled together a plan to get us through the memory-exhausting days ahead. A get-together with Sadie's friends. A weekend away with my husband, and then an overnight visit with my mother. A special dinner with the kids, and a celebration of our grandson and a second brand-new grandchild—another bright gift of light in our midst. Additionally, I was totally pumped about an upcoming educational tour to Israel/Palestine as one of my part-time study courses, just six weeks away. There was so much good in my life, plenty of reciprocal love and nurturing all around.

I'd lean on the Lord and pass by this monstrous one-year marker.

## 45

THE TRIP TO the Middle East was coming up fast.

There was much to do to prepare—tidy up loose ends at work, attend the required theology lectures, complete the course reading prerequisites, and see to household tasks, not to mention pack appropriate clothing and ready myself to address religious sensitivities. Too, my classmates and I were learning a few Hebrew and Arabic phrases. Shalom was by far the easiest to roll off my tongue and, likely, the only one I'd remember.

Preparing my mind for this visit to the land where Jesus walked and where so many Bible stories took place, I had to remind myself, this wasn't a dream. I was actually going! I'd prefer a meditation-type visit, where I could soak in the environment, rather than one scurrying about from site to site, taking notes and preparing discussion papers to meet the professors' requirements.

My colleagues didn't know me well and had no concept of my recent loss. I hid it, not wanting to be seen as a victim of sorts. I was after truth, not empathy. And I hoped a plethora of gleanings would present themselves, the very words of Jesus to my countless God-inspired visions and dreams. More to add to that house of faith I was building.

I knew this was what the Lord wanted too. After all, did he not send me on a counterclockwise journey around that holy cave, returning with God's Word in my hands and my eyes upon its pages?

I thanked him for this opportunity. Though I hoped he didn't look too deep because a sticky grudge just wouldn't dissipate in the hallway of that heart-home of mine, blocking my path to the one-and-only window.

A sinister thought lurked. Christ had never lost a child while he walked on earth, so would he really get how hard this journey was? Birthing one's own flesh and blood came with a deep chasm of unconditional love, a sense of purpose and self-identity that took up residence inside the parent's own body.

Classmates had agreed, the shortest verse in the Bible, "Jesus wept," was one of the most powerful.

I held back my thoughts. If Jesus was truly sad about a dearly loved one's death as a parent over their child, it should have read something like, "Jesus collapsed under the unbearable weight, his bleeding heart beaten with a rod. In his helpless rage, he wanted to scream at God, a piece of him now dead too."

Maybe this trip would help dissolve that lump.

Or maybe, one day, I'd just ask him.

## 46

THE EVENING LECTURES twigged me. From the Israelites wandering in the desert to an entirety of generations who would lose their way to the end of civilization, God saw how all journeys ended before they even started. "I make known the end from the beginning, from ancient times, what is still to come. I say, 'My purpose will stand, and I will do all that I please'" (Isaiah 46:10).

He knew of Sadie's lessened days before she was born. He knew how that would break me. He knew I'd come into the trappings of unforgiving mistrust due to stolen innocence as a child. Did he just watch all of it, knowing in advance it would all happen? Do nothing to stop any of it? How could that be his purpose and pleasure?

I hadn't made peace with this yet. Mind you, I acknowledged he did warn me about Sadie coming home early. That one-two-three vision where God's hand called out the third position to my right, and off went a little girl skipping into the hands of Jesus.

I cringed at the recollection. No way could I stop the drips from my eyes. I'd have to wipe the guilt with the cloth of God's message to the Jewish exiles in Babylon. "'For I know the plans I have for you,' declares the Lord, 'plans to prosper you and not to harm you, plans to give you hope and a future'" (Jeremiah 29:11).

That one-two-three vision was a forewarning of things to come, not a warning of judgment, nor of punishment. Far too much to bear otherwise.

A set of tracks is said to be laid out for each personal journey. Thanks due to plenty of rail-related dreams, I'd been given hints for mine. And thanks also due to the gentle and perceived voice of Sarah McLachlan reminding me to write down my dreams and not to throw them away, I could flip back and forth through my journal to sort them out. There was something there. I was sure of it. Something I needed to study before my trip.

The first time a train and its tracks had entered my mind's eye was in early childhood. Easy to recall, it left me with the horror of feeling abandoned.

I was standing in a field of tall grasses, staring eastward. Not that I would have known what a compass bearing was back then. Train tracks on my left curved off into the distant north. I had just been tossed off and landed on my feet somehow. The only way home was by that train, which left me in its rearview mirror with clear instructions—"Go, walk, and find your way home."

I recalled the hollow feeling the most. Finding my way would be so hard and so very lonely. I was a mere child. What did they expect of me? I'd had no recollection as to where home was, nor even might I recognize it if I did find it. The wild grasses all around me were almost as tall as I was. It was a wheat field. I'd have to stand tiptoe to see where I was going. Bunches of insects crawled around my unprotected feet. I turned, faced westward. And before I could take a step, I awoke.

Strange, huh?

I found the scribbles where I captured another sort of

train-tracked journey, this one in the early stages of Sadie's treatment—

At the end of a railway line were cement blocks planted across the track. Jesus was standing in front of the blockade, smiling, his right hand motioning upward. He was inviting me to see the sunny clearing in the clouds. Several hands reached down from the opening. One large pair of hands, female, plus a few other pairs, were ready to help me up.

That was it.

Since it was brief, I hadn't given this one too much thought, other than the pleasantry that others were helping me along the way. Ancestors, perhaps? Or perhaps it meant the journey I'd been on during Sadie's health challenges was indeed a phase to which all phases end at some time. But now, with the theological renderings, my meditations on Scripture readings, the train and the tracks meant something more. I reread the one most heavily on my mind, the most recent one, after Sadie's passing, and now a clincher with meaning. Something to add to my new foundation of faith.

I was on a train with Sadie. We were traveling north and enjoying the ride. The train stopped for no apparent reason.

Sadie offered to check it out. Then she flew straight out of the front of the carriage and told me to wait. In real life, she'd already passed, and in this dream, she'd already joined her new world, so having such abilities to fly and move through solid walls wasn't strange.

As I waited, though, more people climbed into the carriage. I placed my baggage on Sadie's seat beside me so no one could take her spot. Soon, the train was full, crowded, and we weren't going anywhere. I wondered where Sadie went and was beginning to think she might not come back. But what was up there that stopped the train?

Frustrated with the crowding and lack of personal space, I left the train and popped into the station's gift shop. I would wait there.

As I admired a gold, ornate candle stick holder with several branches, Sadie appeared behind me. "No, no, Mama!" She guided me to a single candlestick, white and plain. "That one."

I bought it, got back on the train, and miraculously reclaimed my still-vacant seat. Sadie had disappeared again, so I'd be making the rest of this trip alone. I removed my baggage from her seat so someone else could sit. Then I faced the window, the east on my right. Nothing but a moist white fog. Like a thick cloud of dew, it smelled so fresh, and I sensed something wonderful, truly sublime and heartwarming, was on that side of the train, delicately wrapped in dense whiteness so eyes couldn't behold its beauty. On the west side, my left, outside the window was colossal chaos, a carnival amped with activity. Roller-coaster rides and all kinds of vendors hawking things. The smell of circus food aroused my senses, but so did the overloaded trash cans.

Last month's ketchup dream! It made sense now—

I left a restaurant, leaving three men at a table. I was supposed to dine with them, but left instead. I went to this outdoor gathering where people congregated and ordered food at a takeout place. They made me fried fish with lots of french fries on top. I wanted ketchup, but when I asked for it, they said, "No ketchup here." They practically scolded me for asking. "You go ask the big boss where the ketchup is." By their smug attitudes, their big boss must be the one who banned it.

The smell of circus food in this dream was the same as the

smell from the ketchup dream. The meaning came together: I'd left the divine threesome in that restaurant to nourish elsewhere, a popular place where Jesus was not welcomed. I equated the ketchup as symbolic of Christ's blood.

All the people on the train wanted to get to that circus. To get there, the train would soon circle left.

And then I knew. That's the route the train was going. But I didn't want to go that way. I was adamant to circle right, a way to that beautiful place representing heaven.

There'd be plenty of ketchup there. I chuckled, breathing in some lightness to such heavy thoughts.

As though in the center of an infinity loop, the left circle—counterclockwise or perhaps westbound was the better description of direction—was the world and all its temptations and craziness, including its beauty and adventurous fun. The right circle—clockwise, let's say eastbound—was the way God told me to turn around that day he promised he'd heal Sadie.

The lecture at the seminary that evening segued seamlessly with my day's musings. It included discussions of the Early Christians and how they were called "followers of the way" in the book of Acts. (Acts 9:2, Acts 19:9, Acts 24:14). "The way" referred to a style of living, of being aligned with Christ's teaching. But also, the path of the way referred to a separation from the world, as it was in my dream.

The circus was the world, and I was to travel in the opposite direction.

At the end of the tracks in that earlier snippet, Christ was there blocking the way. Scripturally known to be the gate to the narrow pathway, he led and warned, "Enter through the narrow gate. For wide is the gate and broad is the road that leads to destruction, and many enter through it. But small is the gate and narrow the road that leads to life, and only a few find it" (Matthew 7:13–14).

I learned that rabbinic tradition held a symbolic meaning too. Clockwise meant alignment, while counterclockwise could be associated with judgment. My mind then drifted in class. That train was my "way." Once, God had told me to circle counterclockwise around the cave where I'd emerged with his Word in my hand. "Stay in the world for now, but listen to my Son" must've been his instruction. Could it be I'd been chastened by God—he'd kicked me off that northbound train and told me to find my way home. Did he do that to everyone?

Bewildered and thinking I'd gone half crazy, I whispered up a thank you. Amazing! God's Spirit had been showing me and teaching me many things throughout my life.

Everyone's train ride would be different. "Whether you turn to the right or to the left, your ears will hear a voice behind you, saying, 'This is the way; walk in it'" (Isaiah 30:21). "I will instruct you and teach you in the way you should go; I will counsel you with my loving eye on you" (Psalm 32:8).

# PART FOUR

*His Holy Land, a playground of purpose.*
*Where his handiwork reveals mysteries,*
*if only we seek them.*

## 47

"I'm a little out of sorts," my mother would say when she felt disconnected without any clear reason why.

That's how I was the first couple of days on this highly anticipated Middle East tour. I'd landed with twenty others at Ben Gurion Airport. Our busload made its way to the first night's accommodation just outside Jerusalem. It was late April, and buds on olive and fig trees were fresh and plentiful everywhere I looked. Despite the continuous threat of war and tempered expectations due to treads of tourism and time, just being there thrilled me, and a tingling of euphoria shot through my spine.

"Can you believe we're here?!" I asked one of my colleagues.

She smiled in return. "I've been here twice already, and I still get awestruck by it all."

I bit my tongue. I wanted to share about my Sadie, her passing, and how even now, here, a shadow of sadness was pulling at my soul.

Sadie's birthday was in a couple of days. Any parent whose child has passed before them is familiar with the sensitivity of such a day. A previous year, my family and I marked it with a brightly iced cake and Sadie's favorite food—chicken fingers and spinach dip. After the feast, we released nineteen pink balloons into the spring air. While eighteen floated away with the breeze, one seemed to defy the wind and head straight up. I watched until it disappeared into the clouds, satisfied that, somehow miraculously, the essence of a gut-wrenching incense had reached Sadie's knowing.

Now, I doubted my decision. It wasn't right to be absent from home, not marking the day. This wasn't fair to my family. Nor Sadie, I supposed.

*I'm sorry you're not getting cake and balloons this year, honey. We'll do it for sure next year.*

That day arrived. I couldn't believe it. Here I was soaking up the sun, sitting on the steps of *the* Temple, facing the Mount of Olives in the distance. Timeless and stirring.

A frozen flood of awe was melting inside me. So many rich stories were tied to the Bible. Embarrassment snuck its way in too. Why didn't I know the narratives better?

There was something about that age of twenty. Scripture verses hinted that to be the age of maturity, a threshold for spiritual responsibility, when God expected one to assume a battle-ready position.

Interesting, given there wasn't much about Jesus at that age. He was just twelve when he sat on these steps and called this temple his Father's house.

I could have sat there all afternoon. I'd have to come back if I ever got the chance. Our tour guide urged us along to their next stop. Snap, snap.

As our group of theology colleagues headed for our bus, a single red balloon floated overhead, then began its climb ever higher and higher, straight over to the Temple courtyard.

My heart lit up.

"Some child must have let it go," the woman beside me said.

"I wonder where they're selling balloons?" Another of my fellow students shaded his eyes and craned around.

Didn't matter. It was a sign. A personal message meant for

me. Sadie's spirit was present and well aware of my birthday wish.

*Hey, baby girl—your balloon! You're here! Happy birthday.*

That evening, when we'd finished dinner in a small dining room set aside for our group, one of the pastors stood up. "Well, all, a special celebration is in order!" He rubbed his hands together in a let's-get-to-it gesture, then winked. "Seems a birthday has been kept secret."

I gripped the edges of my chair, my chest motionless. No one could possibly know today was Sadie's birthday, could they? I'd not said anything. I gulped, unready to be caught so unexpectedly, so emotionally unprepared. It would be like wearing borrowed clothing without proper permission.

The pastor gestured to a table to my right, to a gentleman in our group. "It's Willy's birthday."

Everyone clapped.

Everyone but me, my hand somehow pressed against my thudding chest as the announcement came and relief dropped.

Then out came a vibrant cake, icing dyed with deep hues of several bright colors.

*Oh, Sadie… This couldn't be more perfect.*

Eyes damp, I scooped a bite. With an aromatic forkful of vanilla and almond lifted upward whilst sharing a boisterous shalom with the others, I let go of that pang of guilt for not publicly acknowledging Sadie's birthday.

*Adonai, you're so good at coincidences. Balloons and cake! I adore how you work.*

## 48

The study tour included a review of the three primary religious groups—Christians, Jews, and Muslims—all cultures and beliefs respected. Following the Temple and the Prayer Wall, we visited several other sites over the week, including the places of Christ's birth and crucifixion, Herodian's Palace, and Mary's birthplace, to name a few. As well as the Mount of Precipice, where, as the story goes in Luke 4, Jesus simply walked *right through* the angry crowd, unharmed. This was after the people he'd preached to drove him to a cliff's edge in Nazareth with want to throw him off, a story filled with mystery and speculation. My cheeks twitched from holding in my amusement. So easily, I could imagine Jesus on a skateboard-turned-magic-carpet whisking his soul and spirit out of here!

At each site, my heart was open, my mind curious but guarded. Discernment was something I cautioned. I'd not come to any conclusions as to signs and symbols. Rather, God's handiwork would speak for itself. Subtle, layered, and waiting to be discovered.

When I could, I stepped away from the group. The demanding churn of activity—mini-lectures, itinerary instructions, maneuvers to avoid crowds, note-taking assignments, on-and-off-the-bus scurries, and sometimes even group prayers—all efficiently drowned out God's whispers.

Even here, the world demanded the soul. God's awe dulled by chatter and itineraries.

One morning just before dawn, our group footed the Via Dolorosa, believed to be the way Jesus carried his cross that early morning he was crucified. The route wove through Jerusalem's Old City, flanked by stone buildings and notable stops for prayer and reflection. A somber walk, indeed.

But must we all travel this Way of Sorrow to find him? I certainly had!

Each in the group appeared inward-focused. Little discussion, some with tight lips and labored breathing through their nostrils, others with thoughtfully slow and deliberate steps. I'd never considered my path caring for Sadie to be a "way of suffering," though the one step after the other along this Via Dolorosa swarmed with echoes. The need to stay upright in the quiet space, the calm of the storm. Staying ahead, to pull my daughter through, aching with duty and love and an innate sense of purpose. Were Sadie and Jesus as confident as I was that God would turn their path to allow an escape from such an inevitably harsh and awaiting reality? Or was I just a fool?

When we reached Al-Wad Street, the place where it was demanded of Simon of Cyrene to carry the cross the rest of the way for a weary and depleted Jesus, I recalled my instruction from God for what remained of Sadie's path. It had been clear: Sadie was drained, depleted in every way. I was to scramble around her and push her the rest of the way to the summit. Divine suffering for Sadie was unavoidable, and my duty was to help her bear it. This was God's messaging, a profound symbol of shared suffering. Christ himself, the Son of God, accepted help from human intervention along this walk. Did he doubt God then? Had Sadie?

I couldn't begin to imagine the millions of pilgrims who footed this same uneven and narrow route over the decades, centuries, millennia. Had they perhaps had similar thoughts?

A path of communal suffering.

At the spot marked to acknowledge where Jesus met his mother along the way, a kinship mounted over the artwork of Mary. The conjured image of a dagger dug deep in her heart released subtle quivers, her sorrow for her Son. Simeon, a devout man of God who saw Jesus as a wee babe, had prophesied to Mary: "'And a sword will pierce your own soul too'" (Luke 2:35b).

I returned to my own stabbing vision with such alarming velocity that a fierce thrust panged my heart, all while Jesus sat beside me, remaining calm and taking no action. My own kind of death experienced.

Strange things, those swords and daggers in the Bible. Seemingly symbolic of war and sacrifice, or perhaps when more personal, a piercing truth. Separation from God was equivalent to the death of a soul. Thank heavens for the redemptive version of Matthew 16:25b and its promise: "Whoever loses their life for me will find it."

As the group continued, awareness crept into my mind.

I had still been holding that grudge. Jesus himself hadn't had any children of his own. So how could he know what it felt like to have one of his own flesh and blood suffer and die in his sight? There'd been considerable evidence in his day that many children died in his era. I'd read of numerous remains of youth being uncovered during archaeological pursuits. So why did the Bible hardly speak of such tragedy? Other than noted instances, at least two, when Jesus made them alive again, reversing the parent's sorrow, why didn't Jesus address these specific devastating losses?

So confusing. Harsh, even. Did age not matter when it came to death from God's perspective?

But of course, the great death was God's own child. He instructed the only child he had to die in front of all, so as to open a path, albeit a narrow one, for those wanting to join as sons and daughters.

He was planning a family. One died, so many could come and join.

And when Jesus wept that time in John 11, in all fairness to him, it was more likely he wept given his witness to the deep sorrow his dear friends were experiencing. After all, they couldn't know and believe to the degree he did. The deep human emotions Jesus must have experienced were taking root. He'd also wept bitterly when Peter disowned him three times the night before this walk to his death.

Whatever I felt along my Way of Sorrow scarcely counted by comparison. Nothing could ever compare to God watching his Son weep, be humiliated, rejected by the masses, and suffer as he did. All of it done *on purpose*. And for what? *Us!*

# 49

THE SITE REFERRED to as "The Sacred Pit" sent my stomach tumbling.

A sickening familiarity.

The tour guide's voice resonated with the words of Psalms 88:6, "You have put me in the lowest pit, in the darkest depths."

A hollowed-out cavern, dark and cold, preserved beneath the house of the Caiaphas, the high priest said to have presided over a hasty nighttime trial following Christ's arrest in Gethsemane. A prison not more than seven to ten feet in diameter dug into rock.

The tour guide gestured to two shallow windows at the ceiling. "From there, scholars believe Jesus would have been lowered—or more than likely, thrown—into this pit."

I shivered from the unrelenting coldness, the unescapable claustrophobia, and the unforgiving heartache of abandonment. It mirrored my own pit, a place I'd been tossed to wallow.

"It would have taken ropes and the power of at least two strong guards to pull Jesus up and out of this," the guide continued.

As my colleagues took notes of various scholarly opines of the site, I took the hollowness on a different path. A message to heart. If Jesus needed to be pulled by others to get out of his pit, conceivably, I did too. Though he would be lifted to his execution, while I just needed a lift to carry on with life.

Perhaps it would be best, after all, to reach out to a grief counselor when I returned to Canada. Maybe even read a few of those books. The image of a bound Jesus being hoisted up by others with rope helped me recognize my bindings, the kind made of pride.

The only issue was, as far as I was concerned and though I wanted it, I was not convinced joy was deserved once I was freed. So, could I cope with that? Possibly. Must be why grievers would rather stay, make the pit comfortable as a place to remain. No reason to get out. Stay long enough, and it became one's home. Cozy and familiar, just not free.

My loud exhale caught the attention of the few classmates standing beside me. I needed to quiet down my inner emotions. Admittedly, grief had a physical presence and, at times, must sound like a continuum of sad, exhausted sighs. I coughed a chuckle and apologized.

## 50

LIKE MANY OTHER Christians, I, too, believed the tiny red flowers scattered throughout the grounds of the Garden of Gethsemane were symbolic of Christ's suffering. Crimson petals displayed their purpose through nature—piercing reminders of that dreaded night. "And being in anguish, he prayed more earnestly, and his sweat was like drops of blood falling to the ground" (Luke 22:44).

His soul, that part of which was human, bled.

I thought of Sadie's stress as we called an ambulance for assistance the night she passed.

Might Jesus himself have experienced such inner turmoil that he raised his fist to God like I did in my laundry room? Most likely not. He had the foresight of divine purpose versus human want. How, though, could regular people be fully aware of their divine purpose and to the extent that one went along with an appointed suffering?

Nothing in my readings suggested a complete understanding of God's purpose for any individual. Rather, the theme was obvious: a daily renewal to lean on him, to trust and obey. Though Jesus did make the request for God to reconsider. He, too, was so overwhelmed with anguish that he required divine intervention, an angel to come and strengthen him.

Neither were we required to battle alone.

True strength didn't come from within, an ideology I'd

always believed, a common belief I'd somehow grown up with. Rather, when the rubber hit the road or, reflectively, when one was coasting fast toward that cliff, it wasn't inner strength we needed: it was the strength that came from the divine. That which arrived via that little spirit orb inside.

The many twisty olive trees lent this place a kind of peace. More spirit it was than soul. A place where one acknowledged the kind of soul death requested by God and let that little spirit balloon carry it away. Crushing and uplifting at the same time.

The word *gethsemane* itself came from an Arabic word meaning olive press, this place having been known for its pressing facilities as well as its trees. How symbolic—a body being crushed to expose its filling of God's Spirit, just as when an olive was crushed, its value was in the oil it produced. The rest was discarded, perhaps used for animal feed. "Then the carcasses of this people will become food for the birds and the wild animals, and there will be no one to frighten them away" (Jeremiah 7:33).

Gross. My stomach pulsed, wanting to heave. Must I always have such a pictorial imagination?

A colleague, Tom, was whispering with no one close by.

"Pardon me?" I inquired, certain he was deliberating the scene, even perhaps as I was.

Considerably taller than I was, he glanced down and cocked his head sideways. "I was thinking of Exodus 27:20—'Command the Israelites to bring you clear oil of pressed olives for the light so that the lamps may be kept burning.'"

"Ah, yes, interesting symbolism," I replied.

Perhaps I needed to add a funnel and filter to my illustration, a reminder that daily doses of oil must be poured in for extra boosts. Keep that cup filled. Keep the lights on. Hadn't five of those ten bridesmaids waiting for Christ in the book of Matthew run out of oil?

A short walk did some good. The guide led our group to a higher ridge on this Mount of Olives, the site traditionally known as the last place Jesus stood, at the time, in risen form. Where Christ's apostles witnessed the ascension. "After he said this, he was taken up before their very eyes, and a cloud hid him from their sight" (Acts 1:9).

I grinned at the mental image of that single balloon floating straight up into the clouds on Sadie's nineteenth birthday.

Of course, Jesus ascended! Nothing less would have been expected.

The tour guide carried on with his on-site lecture. When Jesus saw Mary, he warned her not to cling to his then-current state. "Jesus said, 'Do not hold on to me, for I have not yet ascended to the Father'" (John 20:17b).

I took this as another instruction: Do not hang on to past holdings of loved ones. While honoring memories and cherished moments, remember physical death is a time to focus on ascension, for their soul lives on, and recognize them for their new life.

My illustration expanded. Mental notations added for lifting words of encouragement.

# 51

"This," the tour guide said, "has to be the earliest true archway ever found."

This structure, north of Israel near the borders of Syria and Lebanon, motivated me with whispered urgency.

"Nearly twenty feet high," he continued, "it signifies an entrance to a fortified city. Made of mud and volcanic rock, it displays building techniques said to align with the time of Abraham."

"Imagine," Olivia, a twentysomething girl and my assigned roommate, whispered, "from centuries before Christ, here a clay gateway still exists."

"Such symbolism," I agreed. "After all, Scripture speaks frequently of an entryway—a gate, a door, a threshold—to the world of divinity."

"Hmm." She raised a hand to shade her eyes. "And too, the words of Jesus in John 10:9, 'I am the gate; whoever enters through me will be saved.'"

Though Jesus also warned that a time would come when that entrance would be shut. No one further would enter, and the season of mercy would change to a season of judgment. Not a good thing! I considered Luke 13:25a, 13:25c: "Once the owner of the house gets up and closes the door, you will stand outside knocking… But he will answer you, 'I do not know you or where you come from.'"

Could this historical structure represent another of God's mysterious handiworks, a message to seeking passersby that God's kingdom was still accessible, though one day, it would be closed? If ever televised broadcasting announced to the world that this structure known as the Canaanite Gate had finally met its collapse, would that be symbolic of a turned page in God's book?

Not just anyone could enter the promised land. It was reserved for Abraham's descendants, those identified by faith, *not* by birth lineage. "And if you belong to Christ, then you are Abraham's seed, and heirs according to the promise" (Galatians 3:29). Anyone with Christ within would be grafted into the same spiritual family.

Olivia motioned for me to come closer to the group. The site lecture was about to begin.

The tour guide spoke about a sign made of volcanic rock discovered by archaeologists in the same area, its relevance noting a successful conquering of the House of David. While it didn't satisfy many scholars' belief that this area was where the House of David stood, it did provide support the Davidic line existed, the line Jesus had been born into some thousand years after the erection of this entryway. "Jesus the Messiah, the son of David, the son of Abraham" (Matthew 1:1a), a family line of descendants.

I pictured one of those tree-shaped photo collages, the head of the family at the top, children and grandchildren spreading out wide branches as the generations grew. That Tree of Life in the book of Genesis was like God's own ancestral family tree. It's not just that we eat from it—we are grafted into it. A descendant child of God's own ancestral tree. The Everlasting Life family, and there, I imagined, was Sadie's photo on one of the branches.

The symbolization made sense. The archway to God remained open and not sealed shut. Jesus invited *all* to come and follow. He hadn't picked out certain individuals when hanging on the cross to indicate who was invited and who was not. He made it clear—*all* were invited. His Father was wanting to build their family, and he was showing the way. 'Tis the season for mercy, and that door to the Way was still open.

What a horror that day will be when this significant architectural marvel collapses—symbolic of the time of shutting out? No more mercy.

## 52

My classmates were noticing I had a different mission on this tour by comparison when it came to observing and learning.

"You okay?" Olivia nudged me, her eyes bright, her energy youthful. She'd asked a number of times during our tour. I'd often been found drifting in thought or wandering steps away from the group. Coming out of left field, my questions generated curious glances.

I had to give my head a shake—*again*—and wobble up *another* smile. "Yeah, so much to think about. I confess sometimes the lectures demand attention I'm not easily handing over."

She returned the smile. "Sometimes, Hanna, I think you're looking too deep. Seems everywhere we go, you're seeking the metaphors, the allegories, and the symbolic reasonings."

She couldn't be more right. Still, I shrugged. "Just trying to get the most purpose-filled journey."

After all, just what was God telling mankind through this triangular piece of land that was forever in battle? This place he'd shown me in a vision, his finger mapping out my next steps with Sadie, a grueling path.

I'd captured many tidbits, some making sense, some far stretching. I sidled a step closer to her. "I must admit the whole water business in the Golan Heights makes my head spin. Superbly rich in symbolism."

At least in my view anyway.

I hovered my pen over my notebook. How could I even capture all the moving pieces?

We were in the Dan area. Mount Herman, a place with significant biblical events just north of the Sea of Galilee, was mere kilometers away.

My pen began moving even as I spoke to her. "Psalm 133:3 noted that atop this mountain the Lord bestowed his blessings of life everlasting, referring to the 'dew of Herman.'" Dew in the Bible was like refreshment to a weary soul and a provision of blessings for mankind. The gift of everlasting life, of course, being the greatest.

"Hmm." She adjusted her sun visor. "According to many Bible scholars, this mountaintop was the likely place of Jesus's transfiguration, that is, when aligned with geographical and logistical evidence."

If true, then Mount Herman was where God's voice declared, "'This is my Son, whom I love; with him I am well pleased. Listen to Him!'" (Matthew 17:5).

I sighed. "So cool to be right here! What a scene that must have been."

Olivia and I weren't the only ones awed. All eyes in the group were flitting and wide, glimpsing toward the mountainous terrain. We stole a few moments then to offer up thanks through a group prayer.

The tour guide held up a hand. "Again, I must stress the need for those spiritual ears."

Indeed, those three words, a command to listen to Jesus, had been followed with an exclamation mark in the Scriptures. "I wonder..." I muttered, "just who added that punctuation? Did God actually yell so his voice would echo across this land?"

I closed my notebook and hugged it to my chest.

"Your mention of the 'dew from heaven' made me thirsty." Olivia dug two bottled waters from her pack and offered me one. "Too, as it happened, this was believed to be where the 'watchers' made a pact to corrupt humanity according to the Book of Enoch."

I accepted the bottle and uncapped the lid. "That text never made it into the Scriptures."

"True, but according to it, those fallen angels, the bad ones, gathered here."

I wiped my mouth from a trickle of escaping water, then recapped the lid. "No wonder Mount Herman was famous for its supernatural events, not to mention its spiritual importance."

She slid her water bottle back into her pack. Then she cocked her head as if challenging me. "Well, *I* can see no symbolic significance in the ski resort now atop the mount."

Of course, neither could I. Interestingly, though, its slopes were owned by three countries—Israel, Lebanon, and Syria.

But never mind all that. The deeper meaning of it all remained hidden in plain sight.

As my feet sank into the rich soil, I wished I'd worn runners instead of sandals. We'd been given fifteen minutes to wander around the dense brush. I found a large rock, the clicking end of my pen poking at my chin.

So, it began with the plentiful snowfall on Mount Herman's peak, melting the shroud of snowflakes until it cascaded down the mountainside and fed fresh water into the northern head of the Jordan River. Crucial as, in turn, the blessed waters fed the beloved Sea of Galilee. Dew from heaven.

Here was the conflict, though: The base of this same mountain was known for pagan worship and sacrificial offerings. In its day, the grotto at its foot was believed to be the portal to hades, *the* "gates of hell."

"Why," I asked when our guide wandered past, "was this given such a name as the 'gates of hell'?"

He stepped closer, his shadow falling over my sandals as he rocked back on his heels, happy, apparently, to give an answer. "The traditional belief in ancient times of water coming forth from this portal was commonly known and feared for its death-associated darkness."

I doodled inside my notebook. My pen marked my mind's processing, sketching water cascading down a mountain into a pool, while water was shooting up into the same pool from an underground cave.

Might the Sea of Galilee be symbolically contaminated? An invisible mixing of God's dew of everlasting life with the hellish undercurrent of death. Kind of like the Tree of Good and Evil. A mixed-fruit deal.

I shaded my eyes to peer up at the nearby guide again. "So many stories involving the Sea of Galilee. I always envisioned it to be a place of blessing, but perhaps it's not."

He and my colleagues around him offered furrowed brows and twisted mouths. Probably best I keep my analytics of symbolism to myself.

My doodled sketching continued, now capturing the basin before me, a basin collecting waters from two competing sources. Good and evil. Heaven and hell. A contaminated mix where fish swim. Where demons begged to jump into (Mark 5:9–13). Where Jesus walked atop its surface and Peter sank (Matthew 14:25–27).

Perhaps God was showing us what our world here on earth was like—a chaotic mix of good and evil.

Those mixed waters of that symbolic sea fed the Jordan River, which, of course, wound its way south. Those poor fish, if they weren't caught, their only natural exit was southbound via the Jordan River. Then onward to the Dead Sea. Its name suitably earned. No fish could survive there, given the sulfur and high salt concentration. Nor would much else, for that matter. And no surprise for the symbolism of fish.

I liked that metaphor. A simple fish and its journey.

Hadn't Jesus sent his disciples out to fish for people? Like the fish, they unknowingly existed in a deceiving world, eyes unopened to the seeped-in evil mixed about with the good.

Like that dream. "Fried fish with no ketchup."

Curious glances looked my way.

Oops. I'd said *that* aloud.

Despite my blunder, excitement tingled. Possibly more Bible verses would come alive with this water-flow illustration in mind. The water's mystical symbolism ran through my veins, and a pleasing aha smile curved my lips, even though my views weren't likely conventional.

I caught the tail end of the tour guide's seaside lecture. "… Then Jesus aided his disciples in filling their nets with fish. He gave instructions to toss their net to the right of their boat."

There went that reference again—turn to the right.

With that, off we all went, back into the bus and onward to Yardenit, where tourists could still go for riverside baptisms along the Jordan.

I pictured why John the Baptist chose the Jordan River. Symbolically, it made perfect sense. Lest something interrupt the southbound river flow, a traveling fish—symbolic for the soul of man—would meet an inevitable death. His baptisms symbolized a turning direction from sin and the start of a new life. Stop the path one was journeying on and turn around.

"Hah," I whispered. "Go north, my son." Was that from a movie I've seen?

Though rather tough, wouldn't it be? Say you were a fish and suddenly had to travel upstream? Tough to imagine, even for an illustration of symbolism. Perhaps that was by design. It might be easy for some, but a wholehearted, fully-in, turn-around wasn't as simple as it sounded.

"Salmon spawn upstream, do they not?" I asked of Tom. He seemed a safe choice to probe.

"Yeah, actually, funny you ask. You know that has a symbolic meaning to Christianity, right?" He must've caught my eyes widening, for he continued. "It is said that salmon spawning tells the story of purpose, sacrifice, and renewal."

"Why's that?" I had to know.

"Simple." He grinned. I think he was pleased to come into a discussion on this topic of Christian symbolism in nature. "This creature surrenders despite the upstream struggle." He leaned in, his study of my face intent, his broad smile encouraging. "They return to where they came from. Back home to God."

Ah. *Hey, that fit in.* I warmed inside. "Fascinating. Thank you for sharing that."

Once our group arrived along Jordan's shore at the popular site, I hesitated to dip my toes into the waters, though I did. Peer pressure, of course. With this new image conjuring, I could no longer consider the Jordan River's revered waters as blessed. One should be wanting to get out of it, not think it a blessing to step into it!

Immersing in these waters would be symbolic of immersion into the world and all its contamination. Plus, aside from my decidedly metaphorical discovery, given the water's murky and ugly brown color, I didn't want my naked foot in there anyway.

"It's hard to imagine these waters were used by travelers for washing clothes and bathing, isn't it?" The guide smiled at us.

"Surely, the waters were clear back at the time of Christ. Right?" Olivia suggested.

"Imagine," another classmate whispered. "Christ's baptism could have happened right here."

"What a surreal thought," their companion responded.

*Indeed.* After that, I heard little of the shoreside lecture, for the churnings inside my head had elevated. My mind snapped back to a tingling realism.

I had an incorrect perception before this, somehow thinking the waters of baptism symbolically cleaned a person. I'd have to make an adjustment for my new house of faith. It must be the action of "coming out" of the water. For one to want to come out, one would have come to a realization that evil lurked alongside the good.

"It sure is dirty now." Olivia shook waterdrops off her feet as she stepped back.

"But it wasn't the water that cleansed Jesus. And thank heavens for that." Feeling grand about my sense of enlightenment, I announced. I wiped my foot with a towel being handed around, then passed it to her. "If it were, God would have ensured the Jordan River was always flowing with crystal-clean waters, wouldn't he?"

Totally symbolic. One must allow their soul to come out of the world. Live in it, not be of it. Remaining in the waters suggested one was swimming blindly, unaware of the inevitable death ahead. Like a fish, get caught with the knowing hook of Jesus.

Huh, it worked. Not only did all this fit into my skateboard dream, but it also expanded the illustration I was working on, a pictorial house of faith to live within. Located mountainside with a cascading waterfall of blessings, that'd be a lovely addition.

I quirked a grin. *God, you've used this landscape for seekers to find you!* "Speak to the earth, and it will teach you, or let the fish in the sea inform you" (Job 12:8).

So much more to discover.

## 53

"Why don't they ever lock the gates of hell?" A classmate burst out at the group. "Because no one ever tries to break in. They're all trying to break out!"

Jokes abounded as our bus made its way to the next stop—Banias, a lush, forested area traditionally accepted as where the Gates of Hades existed.

"This oughta be a good lecture!" another classmate jested.

Our guide began his site lecture. "This was where Jesus gave a declaration to Simon, whom he had renamed Peter, a name derived from the word *rock* in Hebrew."

A fellow named Peter in our group took a deep bow.

Our guide chuckled. "This Peter was the same guy who sank into the Sea of Galilee due to his 'little faith' and who denied Christ three times before his crucifixion."

What kind of music must've played for Peter from his emotional orchestra to entice him to deny Christ? Something perhaps that made him fear for his own life. The theme from *Jaws* played in my head.

"Here," the guide continued, "is where Jesus was believed to have claimed evil would not prevail. His church would be unshakable. 'And I tell you, you are Peter, and on this rock I will build my church, and the gates of Hades will not overcome it' as stated in Matthew 16:18."

It had been a long day. All I could think of were those two

water sources mixing up invisibly together in a sea of water with Jesus standing on a rock of faith aside it. Hah, with a fishing pole, I'd added for the fun of it. Plus a bottle of ketchup.

That evening, my roomie went out with a friend from class, and I scoured for verses relating to the contaminated evil in waters. Plenty to be found, much relating to the symbolization of a dire need to purify the waters, meaning the fallen world we all swam within. Particularly noting a time yet to come.

While multitudes lurk about in the waters, which John from the book of Revelation suggested indicated people from every nation (Revelation 17:15), the beast rises from the waters, evil at its purest form (Revelation 13:1). But God causes the sea (the multitudes of people within it) to flee and the Jordan River to turn back (in the opposite direction of the inevitable Dead Sea). "The sea looked and fled, the Jordan turned back" (Psalm 114:3). "Then I saw a new heaven and a new earth, for the first heaven and the first earth had passed away, and there was no longer any sea" (Revelation 21:1).

He saved the day.

It could easily be read as a fantasy novel.

One might find the Holy Bible identified with various genre categories in a bookstore—wisdom literature, sacred texts, historical narratives, prophecy, and religion. But fantasy fiction was one shelf this book will not rest upon.

The clarification for the biblical symbolism of seas and rivers aided my understanding considerably. Other than those described as living waters, I began to acknowledge why God insisted these often stunning, peaceful, and beautiful waterways were excluded from the vision of the new heaven and earth that God gave to John the Apostle. The symbolic mixture of good and evil was no longer. Purified. Evil gone.

Pretty cool. And desirable.

And it's no wonder Jesus walked *on* water rather than swam *in* the Sea of Galilee (John 6:19–20) and that the Lord's voice was heard *atop* the waters, not from *within* them (Psalm 29:3). Then the various boat themes, safety found tucked inside a boat despite the stormy seas, and let's not forget Noah's ark. When those waters rose, those in the ark were saved, for they were not left to navigate the waters with simply their human bodies of flesh.

Skateboards sink, remember.

More assuring words flooded as I reread various verses. Such as when God stopped the Jordan River from flowing so the Israelites could pass into the Promised Land (Joshua 3:15–16). Everyone seemed to know that popular story. But the details? It was flooding season, the time of harvest. God stopped the river flow from upstream where a town named Adam existed. He cut off the waters to the Dead Sea. So his people could cross into the land he promised them. Another of God's imagery, a parable of redemption, perhaps even apocalyptic, given the symbolism of harvest to the end times and the saving reversal of the cautionary message "you shall surely die."

And his promise to us, "When you pass through the waters, I will be with you; and when you pass through the rivers, they will not sweep over you" (Isaiah 43:2). He is with us while we are in the world, and he will get us safely to the other side when that certain time comes for each of us to cross that river.

Oh goodness, like a bridge.

My roommate returned, and I turned out the main lights, keeping on only the light over the desk. There was little sleep for me that night, too many ideas buzzed in my head. Particularly, a dream with strong imagery from years ago. Maybe even a couple of decades ago.

How could I have tucked this one away?

A winding footbridge stretched into the horizon, beneath it a deep body of water. The sky was darkening by the second. An utmost urgency to get onto that bridge prevailed because the storm of all storms was coming.

As I ran to the bridge, I approached a small booth at its entrance. Nothing fancy, simply an old-fashioned tollbooth. I had to provide two things: a ticket and a passport.

It was a scramble. I searched my pockets, scolding myself for not keeping those precious items in a better place of safety. Eventually, I found them and passed both along for inspection.

My ticket was wet. As the man examined it, a slight panic rose in my chest. It was still acceptable, so he waved me along.

Interesting. Feeling a bit wiser to God-inspired messages these days, I decided the passport must have meant a kind of evidence—I was who I said I was, and Jesus lived within me. He couldn't be denied passage. He was a permanent resident of the destination.

The ticket must have meant my entry was paid for. It had been a gift, as the cost to enter was well above my personal wealth. The Holy Spirit had made the downpayment, so I was cleared for takeoff, so to speak, it allowed the safe passage the bridge offered *above* the waters.

In that dream, I'd been required to provide both—a passport *and* a ticket.

Hmm, proof of Christ within *and* Spirit-filled.

Jesus must have been quite the salesman in his day, equipped with a solid business strategy. The world was a problem for the people within it, and he claimed to have the only solution. It's likely that people didn't grasp the reality of death and felt little need to seek a solution, let alone believe his was the right one. Change rarely happens, unless the pain of staying the same feels greater than the pain of changing.

It's quite amazing when you think of what he accomplished during his brief ministry, less than four years. A hero in change management. And for this purpose and ever since, God's work continues through his Spirit.

That bridge provided was solid, and many people have already crossed it. Perhaps they flew like graceful doves with wings rather than walked. Or maybe even skipped along it with childlike energy and innocence as Sadie did to Jesus in that vision decades ago.

Before a final eye-rubbing yawn, I discovered there seemed to be a difference between two terms, the *sea* and the *abyss*. It had to be quite the disparity, given that even a legion of demons far preferred to enter into pigs and fall into the Sea of Galilee than be sent to the abyss. In fact, they begged Christ not to order them to the abyss (Luke 8:31).

Well, enough for the night, but not before ruling out some meanderings suggesting the place of hell—the abyss—was intertwined with life on this earth. An easy thing to conclude, given the earth's state with ample doses of war and threats of war, poverty, injustice, grief, and abuse in varying forms. If that was the sea we lived and breathed in, I wouldn't even want to imagine what the abyss could be like. No one could wish that destination upon anyone!

*Sadie, my dear, I am so thankful you are in safe and loving arms. Good night, honey.*

## 54

My stomach had been churning for days now. The more I contemplated, the more I wasn't sure I liked where all this was going. The whole southbound-river-flow business. Though I wished it were all some fantasy, I couldn't deny the way I was gathering wisdom to build a solid foundation and be confident with the solid flooring. Though the walls around me remained like a slippery mud pit, the reliable images I could pull on for reminders of faith and truth would enable me to climb out. In due process.

Patience.

Just as Sadie said, "Just wait, Mama. It'll come."

God hadn't disappointed with false information up to this point. I'd come too far to stop now simply because it seemed unbelievable. Two specific clips from the past, days when alongside Sadie, weighed in—

A beautiful lake scene, so incredibly calm and peaceful. The beach was a half-moon with waves slipping onto the sandy shore, then returning just as lazily. A line of trees so green against a clear blue sky. A relaxing awe from Mother Nature, God's creative fingerprint.

Then things started to change. Quickly, in fact.

The tree line sank into the earth. The water receded. The mud beneath the lake rolled onto the shore and formed a dam before transforming into a flat and broad floor of rock—a floor at towering cliff height. The water's surface lay much lower behind it, though it rebelled and threw angry waves, wanting to overcome the shoreline with its laps once again. That would be impossible with the new image.

A knowing sense revealed the ocean itself had somehow become bottomless. Every atom making up that once beautiful and peaceful scene churned into one of two very distinct components: a solid or a liquid.

A large mass of rock aside a bottomless and angry sea.

Always two.

There always seemed to be two opposing things to compare in many biblical parables—the two trees in Eden, sheep to goats, wheat to tares, grace to law, light to dark, good to evil, Abel to Cain…

Though that latter one seemed rather complex. Why hadn't God looked at Cain's offering, the fruit from his plantings? God had assured him, "If you offer correctly but do not divide correctly, have you not sinned? Be still; his turning shall be toward you, and you shall rule over him" (Genesis 4:7; English translation of the Greek Septuagint). When something didn't make sense, I've learned to go back to the Greek version of the Scriptures and investigate what was originally said.

Perhaps God was referring to the fact that the fruit Cain was offering still contained some mixings of good and evil combined, since it hadn't been divided properly. After all, God did tell him the ground his planted fruit grew from was cursed, and when it came to sacrificial offerings, God wanted only the good. Like wheat and tares, Cain might not have sorted them out at harvest time. Instead, he'd offered up a mixture of both. A sacrifice to be rejected, of course.

Was God also forewarning Cain that the enemy was lurking,

but he would have the strength to overcome it? If that were the case, Cain hadn't trusted the words given to him by God.

He gave up too easily. He chose to feed on the evil growth of his plantings.

Thankfully, there's no concern about dividing sacrifices in this day and age—Christ took care of that on our behalf.

I shook my temple of musings. *Focus. Where was I?*

That dream, the separation of everything in nature into either a solid or a liquid. Always one or the other when it came to choosing. No more mixing of the two.

As if a swiveling platter, I rotated my thoughts, circling back. There was no bridge or tollbooth in this dream. Nothing else, other than the sky, which happened to be blue, clear, and calm. No storm on the horizon either. One could stand upon the rock or, if brave and stubborn, with their own physical strength, remain swimming in the waters below. The latter, an impossible place to survive for any length of time without a solid to rest upon and nothing—or no one—to lift them out.

At the time, I figured God was telling me that all was not what it appeared to be. That I had something to stand upon. That his promise Sadie would live was solid.

The bus was waiting. Time to climb on. Off to the next stop, the Shepherds' Grotto in Bethlehem. Overwhelmed, I sank into a seat. Everything seemed to challenge my personal suffering. Though the grief I harbored often felt more than I believed I was capable of handling, God's messaging through the land and waters here in this special place spoke loud and clear.

I pressed my forehead against the bus window. Why did I believe God *should* be saying, "Suck it up, buttercup"?

My personal suffering was trivial when compared to a much deeper and universal sorrow. And even though sometimes our world felt calm and paradisiacal, we shouldn't be deceived as to what is yet to come.

Would he reverse the process of his creation, push all into chaos? Judgment via returning the earth to a formless, flooded, and dark environment?

The tour guide was giving instructions. We would soon be passing a checkpoint to enter the West Bank. I readied my passport, holding it open to the photo page and peering at the lineup of cars and buses. It could be a long wait. No evidence on these legalistic pages said Jesus lived within. Perhaps in this world that was a good thing—that only God truly knew.

A flash of another past vision, also a brief clip, one that came shortly after Sadie passed, stole my thoughts as the bus tarried in line—

I watched myself sleeping soundly on the couch when an alarm blasted. I awoke and flew—yes, flew—to the front door, reaching out for the handle. There was no time to unclick the lock, and that didn't matter, given my body floated straight through the door. I couldn't get outside fast enough. A black limousine had pulled into our driveway to pick me up. A pastor I knew was driving, my pet dog from years past in the passenger seat.

That was it. The scene disappeared, but it had been an instruction. At least, so I convinced myself. Apocalyptic, maybe. Had that scenario been real, I wouldn't have as much as a half second to get into that car. They—not sure who, perhaps a responsible divine *they*—had come to pick me up, I wasn't to go back and get anything or warn anyone or have one last look. No time for such. Get in the car and get out of Dodge. Though I wouldn't likely be flying, I'd be using my legs to scurry out. Well, who knows? Time might tell.

In Luke 17:32, Jesus warned his disciples, "'Remember Lot's wife'" when explaining the coming of God's kingdom. Just go, don't look back. When angels came to rescue Lot and his family from Sodom before its destruction, that command was made clear. "But Lot's wife looked back, and she became a pillar of salt" (Genesis 19:26).

Which, by the way, several salt pillars exist by the Dead Sea. Of course they would, more symbolism.

Might that happen? Would looking back be a temptation commanding a strong will? Of course, it would be. One would want to be sure their family was coming too.

Would I be smart enough when, or if, that moment came to let my oil-filled spirit take charge? *Don't take no for an answer from my silly, hesitant soul!*

Another reason to give that spirit within the time and nourishment it needed to grow and be replenished.

## 55

Boarding the plane felt good.

I'd collected ample to digest from this study tour. My heart was fully invested in all I took away, though I still found myself battling the logical side of my brain.

Was it my imagination, or had I truly discovered a rich tie-in to several stirrings? Impressions and glimpses of biblical learnings. Quite the untraditional way of learning, though there was no denying the process. Several Scriptures suggest this way of teaching was real. "'But the Advocate, the Holy Spirit, whom the Father will send in my name, will teach you all things and will remind you of everything I have said to you'" (John 14:26).

Still, I'd leave ample room for adjustments. My faith journey wasn't over, and there'd be plenty more to learn.

Our study group headed back home, where I'd appreciate Canadian soil more than ever, thanking God. We are born into the land and into the story he chooses.

Even on the plane, a short snooze left my mind with a vivid image—

I was on a boat, one akin to a fishing boat, though no one was fishing. No motor was required, given the vessel was on some kind of mechanical track that kept it going at a steady pace with no way to stop it and no need for a pilot. All but I were milling about. As for me, I was frantic... absolutely frantic.

Terror-stricken at the back of the boat, I was pointing,

staring at the spot in the water where my daughter had just fallen. She was bobbing up and down on the surface, yet the boat kept on its journey.

No one did anything to help pull her from the waters. No one would stop the boat.

I screamed for it to stop, to turn around. Go back and get her! As the boat motored along at its steady pace, I stared at where she had fallen, horrified as she got tinier and tinier. Eventually, I couldn't see her anymore. I kept my eyes steady, focused on the exact spot in that body of endless waters. I tried to climb over the rails to get to her. People pulled me back, yelling and calling me foolish. I was so insulted, felt so uncared for and disrespected. Eventually, someone coaxed me to turn my head. He walked me to the front of the boat and said, "Watch from here. We go in a full circle. In time, you will see her again."

Of course, this dream was full of symbolism that I was now more familiar with.

Forward-looking was the message. That was where I needed to face. And we are both safe, me in a boat *atop* the waters and continuing my journey, Sadie already lifted up and out. It was her skateboard I'd been watching and frantic about.

A long day of travel and finally, home sweet home. I was disappointed to find grief still lurking in the corners. I'd sensed it as soon as I stepped inside. A blackness still dripped from the walls and smeared the windows, smudging views to keep me inside myself. Energy zapped at each turn of the rooms.

*Oh, Sadie, how I miss you. My heart aches so. I simply cannot help it.*

It took months before I could share much. The hardest thing I'd ever done was to turn from my grief. To unglue my blank gaze at the waters, the view from the back of that boat, and move slowly, hesitantly, forward-bound. Grief was a tough barrier to break through, mentally and emotionally, logically and spiritually. Regardless of how one might analyze it.

All the overwhelming blessings of learning resulted in a gifted ladder. I had climbed up and out of that pit. I sat on the cliff's edge for a long time, feet dangling. But, eventually, I stood, turned from it, and walked away.

To the front of the boat as it sailed atop the waters. Sadie was in my future.

## 56

BE ALL THAT it may with a new home of faith shaping up satisfactorily, a major issue plagued me—

Jake.

That visit from decades ago. The hauntings of a man with an ax and a pleading hand had nothing to do with a biblical message.

Or did it?

Christ's gentle and urgent plea for each to come, follow him, was one of the most critical themes in the Scriptures. Practically the entirety of the New Testament. Simply put, he was the solution that was not readily available in the Old Testament. Nothing else was working, so God pulled out the ultimate measure by sending his Son, whose plea to "come" was central to his purpose. Considering all of God's handiworks—messaging through his creation, through the awe of nature, through tiny and astronomical miracles, through dreams and visions, God is desperate to be seen, to be known, to be heard. His subtle and invisible qualities are representative of his nature, otherworldly with compelling authority. "For since the creation of the world God's invisible qualities—his eternal power and divine nature—have been clearly seen, being understood from what has been made, so that people are without excuse" (Romans 1:20).

Was it possible Jake was not, in fact, Jake? That the man was a divine encounter, and I misread it? A time when God drew near, and I miscalculated?

My mother's words that day spoke volumes, "Are you sure it was Jake?"

What if that had been a visitation from Jesus?

Ouch! The weight of it all felt like a gut punch.

I needed a moment to absorb this flooding wave of enlightenment. But he had an ax. Was that the so-called ax of judgment? Was that my warning? And that old house he stood aside—was that symbolic of my house, the one that didn't stand up to the storm? That hard ground he stood upon with mere patches of healthy growth—the hardness of my heart, perhaps? Threads from a shag carpet?

I hadn't come across much in the Bible by way of clarity for the likes of ghosts, other than references suggesting those who imitate the dead do so to lead one away from the truth. Though there was the transfiguration where Moses and Elijah spoke to Jesus upon Mount Hermon. Plus, Gabriel and that angel at the tomb. So, yeah, spirits are around, to some degree, at some level.

Nothing about Jesus showing up in person with an ax.

But who really knows?

"Dear friends, do not believe every spirit, but test the spirits to see whether they are from God" (1 John 4:1a).

Believing it was Jake for all those years had made logical sense, even though it left a notion of unsettledness. A seed of doubt. Given the story I'd been told, the tragic and traumatic blow my ancestors had been dealt, not to mention the committed threat that all descendants would be killed by an ax, it fit the narrative. Quite perfectly. I had chalked it up as some kind of intergenerational trauma. Like a soul wound passed from womb to womb. Only God could know how that worked.

Was Jake symbolic of a planting within myself, my own mix of evil with good?

My studies of Scripture confirmed a relevant theme: though God may know the future for all, his enemy did not. However, the enemy is acutely aware of the past, and such can be great fodder for accusations or some kind of entrapment. Because of this, God issued a directive in Isaiah 43:18: "Do not dwell on the past."

His Word heals, while history haunts.

Considering that visitor was, indeed, Christ, a true spirit from God, was a message aligned to biblical truths—I'd have to go with it. That fell into the boundaries of rules I'd made for myself. He was pleading and aching for me to come, to follow him.

With dropped shoulders, I let my head shake away the heat from foolishness. It was not some plea for forgiveness for a past crime made to a relative; it was a plea to take Christ's hand, to trust him. Yes, to follow him, straight past the beast.

Perhaps I was drowning in the sea and didn't even know it. Yet, he came to offer his hand.

How could I have known? God had been showing me his story all along, telling me the themes of Scripture. Some would even say the timing for such was ripe. Surely, many others around the world experienced similar. "In the past God spoke… through the prophets, but in these last days he has spoken to us by his Son" (Hebrews 1:1–2a).

Were we not in the early days of the last days?

So then—might those hatchet attacks across the bridge of my nose all those years ago make some sense too? The enemy repeatedly attempting to destroy the spiritual opening of my eyes, to keep them shut, keep me in a blind swimming state.

"The god of this age (the head of all evil) has blinded the minds of unbelievers, so that they cannot see the light of the gospel that displays the glory of Christ, who is the image of God" (2 Corinthians 4:4). Evil's wicked finger muddying up the waters for the great deception.

Though God himself lifted that veil, clarified things, so I could begin to see. He was well-known for taking something intended to harm and turning it around, changing it to a blessing. If the winds of that tornado never lifted me across the steep valley to the right mountain, the one I'd seen in a vision well before Sadie's health was jeopardized, I likely would have continued with a firm belief that Jake from ancestral days had shown up and sought to harm me. My faith might not have moved to the alignment God desired.

And such a result, a failure to see or move, would have been the desire of the enemy.

I'd even misread those gentle whispers I heard as a new young adult—those *marry me* words from Christ.

He must think I am high-maintenance.

Yet, I'd arrived. I'd crossed that chasm by getting out of that pit. Not only was I at a place of stronger faith, but I'd also reached a place of knowing. I now had no doubt of the need of Christ and the bonding with God's Spirit, the coming out of the seas, the grafting into the Tree of Eternal Life, a heart-house built on solid rock. "But whenever anyone turns to the Lord, the veil is taken away" (2 Corinthians 3:16).

I am grateful he left a window slightly open. His ways are definitely not our ways, as they say.

*No kidding!*

## 57

Considering the progress I'd made, much had fallen into place. A blueprint illustration, a secure frame for my house of faith.

Though plenty yet to figure out. And quite a ways to go before the exciting time came for finishing touches. Decorating was always so much more fun!

A big why stirred within me. Why had God chosen me as a recipient for that lifelong lineup of divine messages? Everything came with vital meaning. Was his taking of Sadie the ultimate cost I had to pay? Payment for a debt I owed? No, it couldn't be. Besides, I was no longer indebted; Christ paid that. Still, I had to allow the meandering thought a space to sit so I could swat it dead. Disregard it. Send it away for once and for all.

It was far grander in God's eyes to be blind and have great faith without the benefit of mysterious messages such as he'd gifted me. I couldn't deny, however, that if he hadn't taken Sadie, I might not have taken his communication business quite as seriously.

And he would have known that.

So, if I'd been smarter spiritually right from the get-go in life, would my daughter have lived instead? It took some time, but eventually and likely for self-protective measures, I settled that this was simply God's plan for my life. And for Sadie's.

My mother had even been a witness to this line of thought. "You'll have eighteen precious years," she'd claimed was whispered into her ear from the presence of a man standing behind her when she observed Sadie, her new baby granddaughter, in the hospital's nursery. Only, Mom kept this mysterious encounter secret until the opportune time came to share it months after Sadie's passing.

Inside my heart-home, I sensed a clear path. My wrestling and cleaning behind me, I could now walk to that window at the end of the hall and stand at the sill to marvel at the good in the world. And there was indeed plenty of it.

With a deep reflective sigh, I admitted I'd gotten my answer. That day I pleaded to God while pounding the dirt to plant those tulip bulbs to show me who I was through the child I carried.

And he did. I suppose he, too, pounded the ground. Only the hole he dug was to bury me like a bulb, so after a season, I could grow out of the dirt. I had to die to come alive.

"You are my child." God had said it in so many ways. And as bittersweet as bittersweet could be, that was enough for me. My cup now overflowed.

I might have lived all this vision-and-dream spiritual business in private, but I'd become convinced the story was purposed for many. It had everything:

The contents of creation—rock and seas.

The fall of the misguided—the slyness of evil.

The drowning in a confused world—the opening of eyes.

The promise of hope—the tarry to wait.

The coming of Christ—to awaken one's spirit.

The suffering to follow his way—the wrestling that comes with it.

The pouring in of God's Spirit—the great Helper we cannot do without, and, too, the newness for the uplifted destination of everlasting life.

# PART FIVE

*When dreams grow dim*
*and visions fall silent,*
*faith, trust, and hope rise to illuminate the path ahead.*

## 58

Through the next decade, I continued to carry Sadie close inside my heart along with Christ. Ever throughout waves of intense grief arrived at their will from time to time. Those visions and profound dreams that used to pound their way into my mind churned to simple whispers of remnants that I chased and often could no longer catch. But no need for them anyway. God's Spirit intercedes, that veil more translucent than before. He was never far away, and I sat with him often.

I've cracked open a new journal, not for dreams or visions, nor for thoughts or meanderings. Rather, for a list of reminders to myself. Because to me, being a Christian is an awakening. The battle starts inside. If it doesn't, it's a no-win deal. So much I'd learned. I jotted them with intense scribbling as they downloaded to my mind, and I intend to add new enlightenments as they come. Too, I realized, that the mess of wires that once existed had diminished. I must have pulled tangled wires out without even realizing it. My new journal writings held no particular order or priority.

No longer did I feel lost in a field of wheat! I know now how to get back onto that train and which direction to take, upward, north, and then right. I still chuckle at the directions. Perhaps north was symbolic for God's judgment, the time to give an account. While east, the direction to God's garden. Though I cannot see it, I know it'll be great.

Stand your body straight and tall with all the required participants! Physical self, soul, and awakened spirit, Jesus, Holy Spirit, and God. Alignment counts.

No judging. Ever.

And no more stuffing things beneath a carpet. Promise!

No need to rely solely on inner strength; the greatest strength came externally, from him.

Stay at the front of that boat, atop the waters, enjoy the present, and look forward to an amazing future.

God reaches out to us in so many ways… Use those spiritual eyes and ears to be watchful.

Continue to load with the Holy Spirit's oil; it's an ongoing requirement, like gas for a car, not just a one-day fill-up. It's *the* cup to have overflow.

Take caution when emotions attack and overwhelm. Was some orchestra below playing you? Stop the music. Seek silence and stillness to check.

Look for treasures! They are hidden in oneself, in coincidences. God's handiworks are all over the place, and often when we don't expect them.

God is not one to punish us. He disciplines, however, intervenes sometimes, all for our own good. To get us back on that train heading in the right direction. There's the three t's. Perhaps tests are to determine one's amount of faith, and tribulations are to grow one's faith? Though, he will never tempt us.

Avoid getting caught up in the past. Or anyone's past, for that matter. It's today and tomorrow that count. Just as it's the second death—that possible death of one's soul should it bob around in midair, then fall—that is to be feared. Too, fear happens to be the beginning of wisdom.

When health issues or physical harm arise with anyone

you know, remember, God's top priority is to protect souls, to lessen their weighty darkness, to elevate them, and to get them across that river. More so than to protect the physical bodies, which eventually churn back to dust. At least that's what I think. Maybe that's why sometimes people aren't healed physically or might be taken unexpectedly. What's riding *on* that skateboard matters the most.

My soul orb will not bob up and down when the day of my death comes. I shall be lifted up, thanks to my awakened spirit. Nope, no "duh" looks then!

I am no longer that old woman with many wrinkles! I shall envision my soul as refreshed.

As far as that ax goes, like a branch, I like to imagine I've been hacked away from the Tree of Knowledge of Good and Evil and grafted into the Tree of Everlasting Life. Yes, a good use for that old haunting ax-head.

I have learned to trust and rely on him. That, for me, was tough. I admit. I feel bad that he had to knock me around to get my full attention.

Most importantly, I know who I am. I am a daughter of the greatest creator ever, God, my Adonai.

Jesus sits on my new couch. Plus, now I can get to that window in my heart-home and gaze out. Not only that, I can enjoy God's renewing breath on a regular basis. Ah, the open window.

Sadie, I think about you every day. Somehow, your death gave me a new life.

God gifted me with a precious family tree that keeps growing and a wonderful network of friends, all very special in my life.

## 59

I ALSO FOUND the parable in the book of Matthew—where a man gives his servants differently weighted bags of gold, goes on a long journey, then comes home to see what has been done with the treasure—to be intriguingly relatable. When God gifts one with something, he hopes they have done something to allow his investment to grow. Though each was assigned their purpose, I believe his long-game investment for growth was for that family, for adoring sons and daughters to cherish in the era of life everlasting. A full garden of trees planted by purified waters.

It seems true that he hands out different measures of faith, just like he did with those bags of gold from Romans 12:3c, "In accordance with the faith God has distributed to each of you." He gifts as he wishes. No sense comparing oneself to another. We are called to our work, our journey, equipped with whatever weight of gold we have been given.

I'd been given a special way of learning, one that stemmed from God-breathed messages. One that wounded deep with traumatic loss. That was one *heavy* dose of measurement. God had a very different view—to not only believe in his Son but also to suffer for him was considered a gift (Philippians 1:29).

So, I suppose I'd been trusted with a heavy bag, nearly nothing as others have received, and yet perhaps more than some. When that day comes for me to meet him, my maker, and he inquires of me that inevitable pointed question, "My child, what have you done with all that I gave you?"

Thank heavens I hadn't kept everything buried beneath that carpet.

With great relief, I can say, "Thank you, Adonai. I shared it."

The End

If you've stayed with me through these pages, thank you.

I don't have all the answers, but I do know this — God shows up in many ways. My story is only one among many, but I hope it's reminded you that he is still speaking, still healing, still reaching out. The path isn't always smooth, but his presence is steady, and his voice never fails. And somehow, all those he places along our way, whether we meet them briefly or get to know them deeply, all play a part in shaping us.

Listen and look out the window of your heart and let God's breeze refresh you. The power of the Trinity is always at work.

# ABOUT THE AUTHOR

*Johanna Frank*

Prior to publishing *The Voice I Couldn't Ignore*, a creative nonfiction memoir, Johanna authored three coming-of-age fantasy novels, each recognized for blending whimsical storytelling with deeper, meaningful themes: *Here Lyeth*, *The Gatekeeper's Descendants*, and *Jophiel's Secret*.

Johanna Frank
www.JohannaFrankAuthor.com

www.ingramcontent.com/pod-product-compliance
Lightning Source LLC
Chambersburg PA
CBHW020520080526
44583CB00013B/667